THE BEST OF THE SKY BLUES
MANCHESTER CITY
A-Z

**Written by David Clayton,
Jules Gammond
& Rob Mason**

First published in the UK in 2007. Second edition 2012. Updated and reprinted in 2024.

ISBN: 978 1 78281 9349

© G2 Entertainment Ltd 2024 · www.G2ent.co.uk

PICTURE CREDITS: Action Images, Alamy, Reuters, Getty Images, PA Photos, Wiki Commons.

ACADEMY

Winning Premier League 2 and the Under-18 Premier League National League in style in 2021 illustrated that for all the big money buys in the City first team the production line providing home grown is still in magnificent order. The 7,000 capacity Sportcity is where the Academy sides hone their skills and match play. Enzo Maresca and Carlos Vicens were the men in charge of the Elite Development Squad and the Under 18s in 2020-21.

JADON SANCHO IN
FA YOUTH CUP FINAL
SECOND-LEG ACTION
WITH CHELSEA'S
MASON MOUNT,
APRIL 2017

Maresca played in England for West Bromwich Albion between 1998 and 2000. He went on to list Juventus, Fiorentina, Seville and Olympiacos amongst his playing CV which ended in 2017 at Verona and included 45 appearances and 13 goals for Italy across six age groups from Under 15 to Under 21 level. At City for just the 2020-21 season, after joining from West Ham where he had been assistant manager, Maresca's success at City helped lead to him taking over as manager of Parma.

Vicens is a UEFA Pro-License coach and has a Professional Master degree in Football by FC Barcelona and the National Institute of P.E. He also possesses a Post-graduate degree in High Performance in Football Coaching obtained at the University of Lisbon. Carlos came to Manchester in 2017 originally as the assistant coach to the Under 12s and

13s and has since made similar personal progress to the talented players he has helped.

Since the modern day City Academy was established in 1998 its success has seen it bring through more professional footballers than any other club in the Premier League. Phil Foden, Micah Richards, Kieran Trippier, Jadon Sancho, Kasper Schmeichel and Kelechi Iheanacho are just some of the big names to come through the City system.

PHIL FODEN CELEBRATES SCORING AGAINST EVERTON, MAY 2021

LEFT:
KIERAN TRIPPIER V CHELSEA, 2008 FA YOUTH CUP FINAL FIRST LEG

SERGIO IS THROWN IN THE AIR BY TEAMMATES
AS THEY CELEBRATE WINNING THE PREMIER
LEAGUE AFTER HIS LAST MATCH AT THE ETIHAD
STADIUM AS A CITY PLAYER, MAY 2021

BELOW:
AGUERO CELEBRATES SCORING V ARSENAL
DURING THE FA CUP SEMI FINAL, APRIL 2017

AGUERO

Manchester City's all-time record goal-scorer with a phenomenal 260 goals. These were made up of 43 in Europe, 20 in the FA Cup, eleven in the League Cup, two 'other' goals and 184 in the Premier League. This makes 'Kun' the highest ever non-English Premier League scorer and fourth top Premier League marksman in total. Not only is Sergio City's all-time top-scorer, he also holds that title for Argentina with 41 goals in 100 internationals to June 2021.

At City, Aguero won five Premier League titles, the League Cup six times, the FA Cup, the Community Shield three times and made the last of his 320+70 appearances in the 2021 Champions League final. City Player of the Year in 2012 and 2015 he was named in the PFA Team of the Year three times and was Player of the Month on seven occasions.

It was at the Emirates Stadium in London that Aguero made his full international debut as an 18-year old in September 2006 against Brazil. He went on to play at the FIFA World Cup finals in 2010, 2014 and 2018 as well as the Copa America in 2011, 2015 (when he played in the final), 2016, 2019 and 2021.

Born on 2 June 1988 in Buenos Aires Sergio started with Independiente for whom he debuted when he was only 15 years and 35 days on 5 July 2003. After 23 goals in 54 league games Aguero moved to Europe in May 2006 when Atletico Madrid invested their record fee of €20m. In 2010 he set up both goals as Fulham were defeated 2-1 in the Europa League final and also reached the final of the Copa del Rey in the same season. He then scored one and made one as Inter Milan were beaten when Atletico lifted the UEFA Super Cup.

It was on 28 July 2011 that Sergio signed for City, Madrid almost doubling their money when he was sold for a reported £35m. Almost exactly a decade later on 1 July 2021 he returned to Spain with Barcelona. He had become a City legend with so many goals and so many great moments, but above all he will always be remembered not just at City but in Premier League history for his goal against QPR in the dying seconds of the 2011-12 season. As the ball hit the back of the net the destination of the Premier League Trophy switched from United to City with Sky commentator's Martin Tyler's yelling of, 'Agueroooo!' becoming one of the defining moments of modern day football.

AGUEROOOO'S
TITLE-WINNING LAST
GASP STRIKE AGAINST
QPR, MAY 2102

ALLISON

Brash, loud-mouthed, arrogant but brilliant. Malcolm Allison was a one of a kind football coach who, it is widely acknowledged, was many years ahead of his time. Innovative and tactically brilliant, Big Mal was the perfect foil for the more steadying fatherly figure of Joe Mercer. In July 1965, Mercer approached upcoming Plymouth Argyle boss Allison and offered him the position of head coach at Maine Road.

With a desire to work at a higher level, he accepted and so began one of the most successful management partnerships English football has ever seen. Though the pair were like chalk and cheese, together they were a dream team, steering the Blues to the second Division Championship in their first season and within two years, City were crowned First Division Champions for only the second time in the club's history.

Allison was often in trouble with the authorities for his touchline antics and was banned time and time again by the FA - if Big Mal had something to say, he said it and to hell with the consequences.

Coveted by a host of other clubs - Leeds and Juventus among their number - he felt he needed to be his own man

and in 1972 was given the chance to prove himself by City. Just nine months later, the flamboyant champagne-drinking cigar-smoking manager had left for Crystal Palace, believing he could no longer motivate the City players. In fact, his managing skills could never match his ability on the training ground and in July 1979 he returned for a second spell at the club, but it proved nothing short of disastrous and he was sacked in October 1980. He would manager Crystal Palace, Sporting Lisbon, Yeovil Town, Middlesbrough and Bristol Rovers before retiring.

In his later years, he was never far from his beloved Blues. Malcolm died on October 14, 2010 at the age of 83 and at his funeral had a City scarf draped over his coffin. He once said: "I used to shout that I was the greatest coach in the world." Few, especially the City players and fans who were around in the late 1960s, would disagree.

ARDWICK FC

When the skipper of Gorton Football Club discovered an ideal patch of ground for his team to make their home, the club upped sticks and moved the short distance to Ardwick. With a new ground and neighbourhood, it was agreed it made sense to change the name from Gorton FC to Ardwick FC and a new club was formed.

Under manager Lawrence Furniss, the profile of the team began to rise and Ardwick twice won the Manchester Cup, beating Newton Heath 1-1 in 1891, who later became their cross-town rivals Manchester United.

However, beset by financial problems, in 1893-94 the club was forced into bankruptcy and in 1894 the phoenix that arose from the ashes of Ardwick FC was Manchester City Football Club, thanks in no small way to Secretary Joshua Parlby. City would at least continue to play in Ardwick, and their dilapidated Hyde Road ground, until 1923 when the club relocated to Maine Road.

ATTENDANCES

The 1934 FA Cup tie between Manchester City and Stoke City still holds the record for the biggest crowd in a competitive English match outside games played at Wembley Stadium since the opening of the national stadium. Some 84,569 people were crammed into Maine Road that day to see Eric Brook's solitary goal send City through to the next round. A decade earlier, 76,166 fans packed Maine Road to watch City draw 0-0 with Cardiff City. As late as 1956, two crowds of 76,129 and 70,640 watched the Blues take on Everton and Liverpool respectively in the FA cup.

City would win the trophy that season having no doubt been buoyed by the tremendous support they had received. The Blues' record League crowd was set on 23 February 1935 when 79,491 fans watched City and Arsenal slug out a 1-1 draw.

The lowest crowd on record is 3,000 in 1924 when Nottingham Forest were the visitors and they took full advantage of the sparse surroundings by beating City 3-1. A poor City side attracted just 8,015 people in January, 1964 for a Second Division clash with Swindon Town, the post-war record low.

At the City of Manchester Stadium (currently known as the Etihad Stadium for sponsorship reasons) the record attendance of 54,693 was set in February 2016 for the visit of Leicester City. A £300 million redevelopment programme of the existing North Stand has been approved with the construction of a new hotel, covered fan park for 6,000 people and increased net capacity to 61,474 (allowing for seats blocked off for fan separation). Construction was expected to commence in 2023 and be completed by the end of 2026.

BARNES

Peter Barnes had no fewer than 28 moves but will forever be synonymous with City where he started his career. Having debuted for City away to Manchester United on 9 October 1974 he didn't hang up his boots until 1992-93 when he played for Cliftonville.

Peter played more than 150 games for City scoring 22 times, the most famous of which came as City beat Newcastle United in the 1976 League Cup final. Barnes' last appearance for City came at home to Wolves on 22 September 1987 during a second stint with the club.

Peter won the first 14 of his 22 England caps during his first spell with City, one of his four international goals while a City player coming in a 3-1 Wembley win over Scotland in May 1979.

One of the best out-and-out wingers ever to pay for Manchester City, her terrorised defences for three seasons and was one of the originators of the step over dummy. Influenced by the likes of Mike Summerbee and Rodney Marsh, whom he watched from the terraces as a boy, Barnes had the ability to cross the ball from seemingly impossible angles.

His father Ken was also a legend at Maine Road in the 1950s and was famously dubbed 'the best uncapped wing-half in England'. Barnes senior later became City's chief scout and had to look no further than his own back garden to find an outstanding talent in waiting.

PETER BARNES OPENS THE SCORING IN THE 1976 LEAGUE CUP FINAL 2-1 VICTORY OVER NEWCASTLE UNITED

BELL

Even Kevin de Bruyne, David Silva or Sergio Aguero would struggle to rival Colin Bell when the accolade of City's greatest ever player is considered. During Colin's era at City, which lasted from 16 March 1966 to 10 April 1980, the club enjoyed a golden era when they won Division Two, the league title, the FA Cup, the League Cup and Charity Shield twice each and the European Cup Winners' Cup. Mike Summerbee, Francis Lee and Alan Oakes were amongst the great players in that side but undoubtedly Colin was the king-pin.

Bell had everything. He was the perfect box to box midfielder. His vision and ability to open up defences combined with his pace, willingness to bolster the defence and ability to score all came wrapped up with the bonus that he possessed the most supreme stamina. Nowadays teams are often rotated and key players are frequently substituted when games look as if they are safely won. In Bell's day substitutes had just been introduced and there was only one, so almost always a starting appearance meant a full 90 minutes. Additionally, factor in that there were four more league games at the top level than there are now, often on heavy pitches and in an era when tackling could be much more aggressive than is allowed in modern day football. Through all this Colin was ever present in the league in 1966-67 and 1974-75, missed just one game in 1973-74 and in a spell of eight seasons topped 40 appearances seven times with three of those campaigns seeing him play between 50 and 55 times. In total his 491+3 games for the club places him fifth in the all-time list while his 152 goals had only been bettered by two players when Colin left - despite him not being a striker.

Colin was capped 48 times while with City, scoring nine goals. Debuting against Sweden at Wembley in May 1968 his first goal came against Brazil in Rio the following year. Bell played against Brazil again in one of three appearances he made at the 1970 FIFA World Cup finals and captained his country against Northern Ireland at Wembley in 1972.

Born in Cold Hesleden near Sunderland on 26 February 1946, Bell began with Bury in 1963 scoring 25 goals in 63 league games for the Shakers before a fee of £47,500 brought him to Maine Road. Undoubtedly he would have played well over 500 games but for missing almost two years after an horrendous injury sustained in a League Cup derby with Manchester United in November 1975. He was not able to play at all in 1975-76 when City finished a point behind champions Liverpool. Had Colin been fit then that season may well have been a title winning year.

Understandably he was not the same player after fighting back from his knee injury and finished his career in the USA where he played five NASL games for San Jose Earthquakes who he signed for on 10 April 1980.

Nicknamed, 'Nijinsky' after one of the greatest racehorses of all time, who was dominating that sport whilst Bell was playing, Colin had the West Stand of what is now the Etihad Stadium named in his honour in 2004 and was entered into English Football's Hall of Fame the following year when he was also awarded the MBE. He passed away on 5 January 2021, shortly before what would have been his 75th birthday.

BOND

John Bond arrived at Maine Road in October 1980 to pick up the pieces of Malcolm Allison's whirlwind second stay as City boss. Having achieved success at Bournemouth and Norwich City, the flamboyant but highly regarded Bond left the tranquil surrounds of Carrow Road for the crisis-torn Blues. Within weeks, Bond had transformed a doomed side into a team worthy of a top three place.

Few managers have had such an instant effect on a side and after watching his troops from the stand lose 1-0 to Birmingham, a result that left City bottom with no wins in 12, he inspired the players to produce a stirring 3-1 win over Spurs just four days later and the juggernaut was off and running. Only a linesman's flag denied City a place in the League Cup Final that season and only a coat of paint saved Spurs in the FA Cup Final as Bond's City became the nations' premier cup team. Signings such as Gerry Gow, Bobby McDonald and Tommy Hutchison combined to play the best football of their careers and inspire the rest of the side to greater heights, and the side that had looked like relegation bankers ended in twelfth spot.

The following campaign saw the arrival of Trevor Francis for £1.2 million and caused great excitement among supporters. The Blues went into the New Year at the top of the table, with many believing the seemingly impossible quest for the league title might just happen. It didn't, and a dramatic slump in form would eventually see City finish tenth.

Bond lasted just over five months of the 1982-83 season with his magic aura fading by the week and he resigned after a 4-0 FA Cup fourth round defeat at Brighton and Hove Albion and four months later the Blues were relegated. His son Kevin played for his father at City amassing more than 100 games for the club before leaving to join Southampton. John Bond passed away on 25 September 2012, aged 79.

BOOK

Few men have served Manchester City with greater distinction than Tony Book, first as captain of one of the greatest City teams of all time, then as manager from 1974 to 1979. 'Skip' joined City from Plymouth Argyle in 1966 for £17,000. Malcolm Allison who had managed Book at both Bath and Plymouth, persuaded Joe Mercer that despite Book being 30 years old, he was one of the finest defenders in the country. All this from a player who had just two years earlier been playing for non-league Bath and brick-laying part time.

Book was made captain and was soon lifting the league championship, League Cup and FA Cup as well as being voted City's first ever Player of the Year in 1967. One of the quickest defenders around, George Best is quoted as listing Book as his most difficult opponent and he was voted joint Footballer of the Year in 1969 as his fellow professionals acknowledged his tremendous achievements over the past seasons.

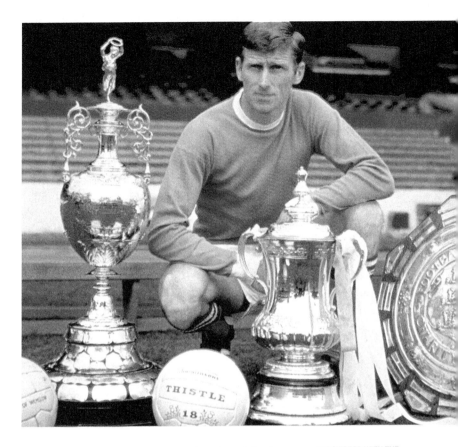

Malcolm Allison said Book was one of the best defenders he'd ever seen and few who saw him play with disagree with that view. Tony captained City to another trophy in 1970, the European Cup Winners Cup and he officially retired in 1974 in order to become assistant to Ron Saunders. He became manager not long after, taking City to League Cup glory at Wembley in 1976 and within a point of the first division title in 1976-77 before being replaced, somewhat ironically, by Malcolm Allison in 1979.

He later became part of the backroom staff at Maine Road for several more years. As a captain and as a manager, Book gave the Blues tremendous service, which stretch over an incredible 30 years.

THE SKIPPER WITH THE LEAGUE CHAMPIONSHIP, FA CUP & CHARITY SHIELD TROPHIES, MAY 1969

BROOK

Eric Brook's 177 goals for City before World War Two made him the club's record scorer, a record only Sergio Aguero has surpassed. That is even more impressive when it is noted that Brook was a winger! Born at Dolcliffe Common in Mexborough on 27 November 1907 Eric played for four local teams before Barnsley paid £200 to sign him from Wath Athletic in February 1926. The Tykes made a £3,800 profit when they sold him to City on 16 March 1928 after 18 goals in 78 league games. City also signed Fred Tilson at the same time, the latter being valued at £2,000 in what was reported as a combined £6,000 fee. There was an immediate reward as City strode to promotion.

Brook went on to play 493 games for Manchester City, his 177 goals being made up of 158 in the league and 19 in the FA Cup - those competitions being the only ones available in those days. Eric debuted at home to Grimsby on 17 March 1928 and played his last match on 10 April 1939 at home to Bury. After a car crash in which he suffered a fractured skull he announced his retirement in October 1940, by which time the Football League had ground to a halt due to World War Two.

Eric played in the FA Cup finals of 1933 and 1934, being a winner against Portsmouth after missing out against Everton. In front of a record crowd of 84,569 in the quarter-final against Stoke Brook netted one of the greatest goals in the club's history with a swerving shot from the right flank. Brook packed a powerful shot and was a top forward who liked to pop up all over the forward line but he liked to stop goals as well. In the days before substitutes he went in goal three times!

In 1936-37 as City won the league for the first time - and indeed the only time before 1969 - Brook was ever present scoring 20 goals, including a brace in the game the title was sealed against Sheffield Wednesday.

All 18 of Eric's England caps came while he was with City. He scored in half of these games, his total of 10 goals including two against Italy in November 1934. Brook passed away in March 1965. He is a member of the City Hall of Fame and was one of 11 players to have streets named after them by Manchester City Council in 1977.

BUSBY

**It was at Manchester City, not Manchester United
that the great Sir Matt Busby first made his name in
England. The young Lanarkshire-born Scot was all set
to relocate to America with his widowed mother until
City boss Peter Hodge persuaded him to stay and sign
for the Blues in 1928, changing his life forever.**

Originally an inside forward, City adapted Busby into
a classy half-back and in 1933 he went on to win his one
and only Scotland cap. He helped City win the FA Cup in
1934 having been a Wembley loser with the Blues a year
earlier. In 1936, after eight years solid service and 226
appearances, Matt Busby was sold to Liverpool for £8,000
and played in one of the Anfield club's best ever half-back
lines with fellow Scots Bradshaw and McDougal.

He later became boss at Old Trafford, moulding an exciting
young team together dubbed 'The Busby Babes' before
the team were involved in a tragic air crash in Munich in
February 1958. Busby survived and guided United to
European Cup glory in 1968 before retiring. He ever forgot
his Maine Road roots, however, and had many friends at
Man City, including Joe Mercer. Sir Matt passed away on
20 January 1994 at the age of 84.

CAPTAINS

City have had some inspirational leaders on the pitch over years from Billy Meredith who was the first captain to lift the FA Cup after a 1-0 win over Bolton Wanderers in 1904. Sam Cowan captained City to three FA Cup finals and Sam Barkas led the Blues to the 1946-47 Second Division title.

One of the toughest and most determined skippers was Welsh central defender Roy Paul who drove his side to success in the mid-fifties with the threat of a clip on the nose if they didn't pull their weight. This was in evidence as City returned to pick up the FA Cup in 1956 after being beaten at the same stage a year earlier. Paul had vowed to take his team back and win the trophy the following season just as Sam Cowan had done 22 years earlier.

Tony Book came to the club from Plymouth Argyle in 1966 when he was nearly 32 but went on to play over 300 games, be joint-winner of the Footballer of the Year award in 1969 and captained City to European glory in the Cup Winners' Cup as well as lifting all three domestic trophies. Mike Doyle then skippered City when the League Cup was won in 1976 and remained the last trophy winning captain until Carlos Tevez lifted the FA Cup after Stoke City were beaten in the 2011 final.

Taking over from Tevez, Vincent Kompany became the club's most successful skipper. He inspired City to four Premier League titles in 2012, 2014, 2018 and 2019 when the domestic treble was won. In the case of the League Cup it was the fourth time the trophy had come to City while Kompany was captain having also won it in 2018, 2016 and 2014. On the first of those occasions Vincent's brilliant tackle on Sunderland's Fabio Borini prevented the Italian doubling the lead he had already given the Wearsiders. Add to all this the Community Shield in 2012 and 2018 and Kompany is unquestionably City's most successful captain.

The brilliant Belgian passed the baton to David Silva who lifted the League Cup in 2020 before Fernandinho took over and retained the trophy in 2021 when the Premier League was also claimed once again. Ilkay Gündogan took over leading the club to a celebrated treble of Champions League, FA Cup and Premier League in 2023 before moving on to Barcelona.

ILKAY GUNDOGAN WITH THE PREMIER LEAGUE TROPHY, MAY 2023

LEFT:
VINCENT KOMPANY LIFTS THE BARCLAYS PREMIER LEAGUE TROPHY AFTER VICTORY OVER QPR, MAY 2012

CELEBRITIES

The Gallagher brothers from Oasis, Johnny Marr, Badly Drawn Boy, Rick Wakeman, Mike Pickering, Mark E Smith of The Fall and Take That's Jason Orange are all city fans as was legendary Joy Division front man Ian Curtis.

Olympic swimmer James Hickman, England rugby union stars Will Greenwood and Andy Farrell, world champion boxer Ricky Hatton, plus rugby league star all make for an impressive list of sport fans.

Comedians Eddie Large, Jason Manford and Bernard Manning, actors Timothy Dalton, Warren Clarke, David Hasselhoff, Michelle Keegan, Alan Rickman and David Threlfall, DJ's Mary Anne Hobbs, and Mark Radcliffe, newsreader Clive Myrie, G2 publisher Edward Adams and money saving expert Martin Lewis, and even apparently Princess Beatrice of York are all City fans.

CHAMPIONS LEAGUE

Champions League victors in 2023 when Internazionale were beaten by a Rodri goal in Istanbul, City reached their first Champions League final in 2021. While that showpiece occasion in Porto ended in disappointment with a 1-0 defeat to Chelsea, reaching the final was an important step for the club in the tenth successive season City had taken part in the continent's top competition.

Having first taken part in the original European Cup in 1968-69, when there was a first round exit at the hands of Fenerbache of Turkey, City were regulars in European football in the 1970s but didn't play at that level between 1979 and 2003-04 when a UEFA Cup place was obtained via the Fair Play League. There were two more excursions into the UEFA Cup / Europa League before a first ever qualification for the Champions League in 2011-12.

The opening game then saw Aleksandar Kolarov score City's first Champions League goal as they came from behind to earn a home draw with Napoli. There was then a 2-0 defeat at Bayern Munich before back to back victories against Villareal, an injury time Sergio Aguero goal proving to be City's first winner in the competition.

Defeat at Napoli meant that even after beating Bayern in Manchester, City finished third in their group after which they moved into the Europa League where they eventually succumbed to Sporting Lisbon on away goals.

City first progressed beyond the Champions League group stage at the third attempt in 2013-14, losing out to Barcelona in the Round of 16 with exactly the same happening the following season, Barca winning all four games. In 2015-16 Spanish opposition again ended City's run but this time the boys had gone as far as the semi-final, where just one goal over the two legs saw City edged out by Real Madrid.

RODRI CELEBRATES HIS CHAMPIONS LEAGUE WINNING GOAL

Now major players on the Champions League scene City are European champions in 2023 and having been finalists twice already in the 2020s City have now joined the top tier of European footballing royalty.

COLOURS

The most successful and famous British club to wear light blue, the colours that inspire 'Blue Moon' haven't always been worn. Originally as Gorton, the club wore black and white with a large white cross on a black shirt. Most likely this was due to the side originally being a church team.

Light blue was introduced to the kit when the club became known as Ardwick, but so was dark blue in halved shirts in the style now associated with Blackburn Rovers. That progressed to light blue and white halves, after which all white shirts were used before an all light blue top was worn for the first time after the club changed its name to Manchester City in 1884.

Since then there have been the tweaks and changes you would expect, particularly in the modern era when kits change each season, but essentially the traditions of Manchester City have ensured that the strip has remained what you would expect, a light blue shirt, classically combined with white shorts and mainly light blue socks.

CORRIGAN

Goalkeeper Joe Corrigan or 'Big Joe' as he was affectionately known at Maine Road, played an astonishing 592 times for the club in a period stretching back 17 years. He signed as a junior from Sale FC and had to fight hard to establish himself as City's number one with the experienced duo of Ken Mulhearn and Harry Down ahead of him in the pecking order.

His early days were fraught with anguish and he was anything but a crowd favourite as he struggled with his form, confidence and weight. His inconsistency led to him being transfer-listed in 1974 but Joe was determined to prove the doubters wrong. He buckled down, lost the excess pounds and improved to such an extent that he was called up to the England squad not long after and surely would have been a regular first choice had he not had Peter Shilton and Ray Clemence in front of him. He won nine England caps in total but played 10 times for the England 'B' team and represented his country at Under-21 and Under-23 levels.

The fans at Maine Road were in no doubt about Corrigan's qualities and they voted him Player of the Year in 1976, 1978 and 1980 - a record number of awards to this day.

With the emergence of Alex Williams and the lure of a fresh challenge overseas, he left City in 1983 to join Seattle Sounders in the USA but returned to play for Brighton and Hove Albion not long afterwards. On his return to Maine Road with The Seagulls, he was afforded a hero's welcome with the fans giving him a standing ovation that lasted several minutes.

A neck injury forced him to retire in 1985 and after hanging up his playing gloves he became a goalkeeping coach at several clubs before quitting the game in 2011.

COWAN

Sam Cowan joined City in **1924** and served the club with great distinction for more than a decade. He captained the side in the **1933** FA Cup Final after telling King George **V** that his team would be "back next year to win it". Sure enough, the Blues returned to win the trophy just as he had predicted and his place amongst the club's all-time greats was assured. He left City in **1935** after playing for Bradford City and Brighton and Hove Albion, settled in Hove, East Sussex.

He became coach at Brighton and set up a successful physiotherapy practice near to the Seagulls' home ground in Hove. City asked if he would like to become the team manager in 1946 and Cowan, although living near Brighton, accepted but commuted to Manchester rather than return permanently. He guided the Blues to the division two title and looked set for a successful career in management but his travelling meant the position became impossible for him and he decided he's rather devote himself full time to his practice on the south coast. How successful Cowan might have been as a manager, one can only guess but he was a born winner and losing him was a huge blow for the Blues.

CRICKETERS

There have been two City players that were also first-class cricketers. 'Patsy' Hendren played 51 test matches for England and scored over 40,000 runs for Middlesex. The well-built winger played only twice for the Blues during the 1908-09 season, clearly showing that his chief talent was as a batsman.

Jack Dyson was a talented all-rounder for Lancashire scoring 4,433 runs and taking 161 wickets between 1954 and 1964. As one sporting season ended, the other began so holidays were a thing of fancy until his retirement from football. He played 72 games for City (1951-61) in all competitions and scored 29 goals, including one in the 1956 FA Cup final. Continuing the theme, cricketers Andrew Flintoff, Matthew Maynard and Phil DeFreitas are all ardent City fans.

MIDDLESEX'S PATSY HENDREN PULLS THE BALL TO THE BOUNDARY

LEFT:
ENGLAND CRICKETER ANDREW FLINTOFF

CROSSAN

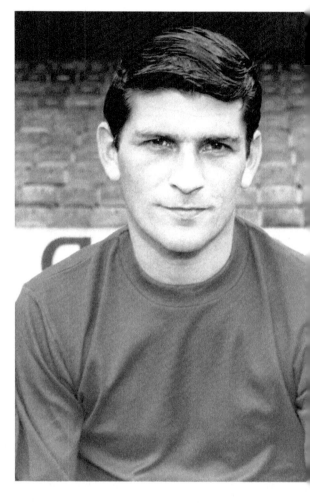

Johnny Crossan's path to Manchester City is quite a story in itself. Following irregularities in a transfer deal taking Crossan from Coleraine to Bristol City, the authorities attached a sin die ban on the talented midfielder. He was left with no other choice but to seek a career on the continent and he was snapped up by Sparta Rotterdam after he impressed at a trial for the Dutch side. He then moved on to Standard Liege in Belgium, playing in the European Cup during his time abroad. His skill and technique were taking on new dimensions and when the ban in the UK was lifted in 1962, Sunderland moved the quickest and snapped up the Northern Irish international for £28,000

He proved a popular signing for the Roker Park faithful becoming top scorer in their first promotion season of 1963-64. City manager Joe Mercer was impressed and made him one of his first signings paying £40,000 for his services. Mercer saw Crossan as the man who could help knit a talented young side together with his skill and experience. He was made captain, a role he revelled in, and City duly won the Division Two Championship. Crossan's contribution was immense, missing just two league games all season and netting 13 goals.

Crossan was a hugely popular figure at Maine Road - skilful and feisty in the challenge, he had a heart as big as a lion and didn't suffer fools gladly. After being involved in a car crash, he continued playing while being hampered by a leg injury and told nobody at the club about his injury. Many mistook his laboured performances for laziness and some of the crowd showed their displeasure and a move away from the club became inevitable. At the end of the season, Crossan was once again on the move, this time to Middlesbrough for £34,500.

DE BRUYNE

Kevin De Bruyne must come as close as anyone to rivalling Colin Bell as City's finest ever footballer. His all round play made him arguably the best midfielder in the world at his peak.

When he was in Germany with VfL Wolfsburg, Kevin was named Bundesliga Young Player of the Year in 2012-13 and Bundesliga Player of the Year two years later when he was also being named the Footballer of the Year in Germany and Belgian Sportsman of the Year. These individual accolades are just some of the honours bestowed upon De Bruyne who up to 2023 had also won five Premier League titles with City as well as playing in four consecutive League Cup final victories from 2018 onwards. On top of all this Kevin also scored in the emphatic 6-0 win over Watford in the 2019 FA Cup final.

With Wolfsburg he won the German Cup, the DFB-Pokal and the DFL Supercup, both in 2015, while with Genk in his native Belgium in 2010-11 he did the double of Pro-League title and Supercup two years after picking up his first senior medal as an unused substitute when Genk beat Mechelen in the Belgian Cup final.

Kevin made his full international debut in August 2010 and won his 84th cap at the quarter-final of the delayed Euro 2020 tournament in 2021. He scored against the USA at the 2014 FIFA World Cup and in the quarter-final of the 2018 World Cup against Brazil before helping his country defeat England in the match for third place. Increasingly troubled by injuries in recent seasons De Bruyne played through the pain barrier at Euro '2020' and will hope to be at his best in his remaining seasons with City and Belgium. Having to go off injured in the Champions League finals of both 2021 and 2023 was tough luck on Kevin but it will help give him extra motivation for another final in City colours when hopefully Kevin can stay fit to show his supreme ability on the biggest stage.

DERBIES

You have to go all the way back to **12 November 1881** to find the first time the two **Manchester** rivals met. Back then City were called **St Marks (of West Gorton)** while United were **Newton Heath LYR**, with **Newton Heath winning 3-0**. The clubs first met in the league on **3 November 1894**. On that occasion **Billy Meredith scored twice for City** but it was to no avail as the visitors - still called Newton Heath - **won 5-2.**

City's first league win came on Newton Heath's next visit on 7 December 1895 when Meredith was joined on the score-sheet by Robert Hill as City won 2-1. In total to the start of the 2023-24 season City had won 59 times to United's 77 with 53 games drawn. In the League alone there had been 52 draws, 50 Blues wins and 66 Reds victories while in 2023 the first all Manchester FA Cup

final saw City win 2-1. Great City victories include a 6-3 win with Phil Foden and Erling Haaland hat-tricks in October 2022. Eleven years earlier two late goals from Edin Dzeko and an injury time strike from David Silva helped towards a 6-1 win at Old Trafford.

That 6-1 away scoreline had also been achieved on 23 January 1926 when Billy Austin and Frank Roberts got two each, while in February 1955 Paddy Fagan and Joe Hayes notched braces as City won 5-0 at United. However perhaps the most famous derby win for City was won by just one goal. That came on 27 April 1974 when United legend Denis Law's impudent back-heel condemned the Reds to relegation at Old Trafford. United fans invaded the pitch to get the match abandoned but to their chagrin the score-line stood. In fact, due to results elsewhere United would have gone down even if they had won.

DEYNA

The 1978 World Cup in Argentina created much excitement in England, particularly when it was rumoured that some of the top names in the tournament might be heading to the Premier League. City fans were delighted to learn that the Blues were on the trail of 102-times Polish World Cup captain Kaziu Deyna, a massive star of Iron Curtain football.

Red tape and the player's involvement in the Polish army would initially delay the deal before a fee of £100,000 was agreed with Legia Warsaw. The Polish side asked City if they could pay the fee in the form of electronic goods such as copiers and fax machines, which they duly did. But though Deyna was undoubtedly a precocious talent, things never really ran smoothly during his time in Manchester.

He was forced to look after his young son alone with his wife hospitalised in Poland for a lengthy period and it wasn't until he'd been with the club nine months at City that he finally found the back of the net.

Despite this, the technique, skill and vision Deyna possessed made him a huge favourite with the City faithful and his first-season return of six goals in 11 starts promised even better to come for the following campaign. Beset by injuries and off-field problems, however, Deyna missed half of the campaign because of one reason or another and in January 1981, he left for San Diego in the NASL. Tragically, he was killed in a car crash in California in September 1989. His elegance and ability have ensured he is fondly remembered at Maine Road.

DICKOV

The £800,000 capture from Arsenal set about terrorising defenders from the word go and what he lacked in height and natural ability, he made up for in sheer guts and effort. He never really enjoyed the luxury of being an automatic first choice but his attitude did not waiver and once her pulled on the laser-blue jersey the five foot five inches pocket dynamo became like a man possessed, chasing lost causes and wearing down defenders both physically and mentally be never giving them a moment's piece.

Dickov's role in helping City recover from the shock of finding themselves in mid-table in the nation's third division and heading for obscurity to the Premiership within the space of 18 months, should never be under estimated and he was the catalyst that helped propel the Blues back to the top division.

It was Dickov whose late equaliser in the play-off semi-final first leg with Wigan Atheltic in 1999 ensured the Blues were on level pegging for the return games and, unforgettably, it was Dickov who changed the fate of City with a truly incredible last-gasp equaliser against Gillingham in the final that would eventually see the Blues win on penalties.

He also sealed the promotion-clinching victory at Blackburn Rovers by scoring the final goal in a 4-1 win as City stormed back to the Premiership a year later. Though his goals were crucial, his endeavour and attitude also helped earn many more points along the way. In a survey of Premiership defenders, both John Terry and Rio Ferdinand cited Dickov as one of their most difficult opponents.

He moved to Leicester in 2002 after failing to hold down a first-team spot under Kevin Keegan and later moved to Blackburn Rovers. In 2006, he made an emotional return to the club he'd become part of the folklore at, and played 19 more times without adding to his scoring tally. He was capped 10 times by Scotland and after hanging up his playing boots later managed Oldham Athletic and Doncaster Rovers. Dickov now works as a television pundit, appropriately for Manchester City TV.

DISTIN

Sylvian Distin deserves his place among the very best defenders to have represented Manchester City. The tall Frenchman joined the Blues for a £4 million fee in June 2002 and in doing so became the club's most expensive defensive signing. Distin had spent much of the 2001-02 season on loan at Newcastle from Paris St Germain but when the Magpies dithered over a permanent deal, Kevin Keegan moved in with a firm bid and secured the services of one of France's best uncapped players.

A quick powerful player at six foot four inches tall, Distin was something of a man mountain and became consistently one of the club's best players. He skippered the side between 2003 and 2005 and formed a terrific partnership with Richard Dunne at the heart of the Blues' defence. Relatively injury free during his time with City, his lung-bursting runs and energetic style made him one of the most exciting players in the country.

Distin left City at the end of his contract in May 2007 and joined Portsmouth where he won his only major English trophy, the 2008 FA Cup. In August 2009, he signed for Everton and over the next six years made some 174 appearances including his 402nd appearance in the Premier League - more than any other foreign outfield player. In May 2014, Distin humorously announced his international retirement on Twitter, calling his record of 0 caps for France as a "wonderful experience".

DOHERTY

The treasured image of a million cigarette cards and a true Roy of the Rovers figure, Peter Doherty, old timers will tell you, was one of the greatest players ever to have played for Manchester City. Though he was at Maine Road for a decade, seven of those years were during wartime and his 133 appearances amounted to a mere fraction of the amount he would have made had he played at almost any other time for the club.

Born in Magherafelt, Republic of Ireland, the tall inside forward became one of football's hottest properties while playing for Glentoran and it was City and Blackpool who put firm offers in with the Blues just edging the battle for his signature at a cost of £10,000 - then a club record. He soon became one of the legends of the game and was also a master tactician on the pitch. Doherty excelled at dribbling, tackling, passing and heading and had virtually every asset a player could wish for. He also delighted the City fans with his endless energy. Doherty was the star of the Championship-winning side of 1936-37, scoring 32 goals in 45 matches. Despite the success and talent of the team, City followed up the League title with relegation - despite scoring more goals than anyone else had

managed! The outbreak of war meant no competition for seven years, though he still played 89 times scoring 60 goals during wartime for the club. If those were added to his official total, he would have scored 141 goals in just 222 games. He occasionally turned out for other sides during the war and it was City's refusal to allow him to play for Derby in a cup match that made him quit the club almost as soon as war has ended. Peter died in April 1990 and a commemorative plaque was unveiled in his native Ireland several years ago.

DUNNE

If City had known just how much of an inspirational figure Richard Dunne would have become wearing the light blue of Manchester City, it's likely they would have played triple the original £3.5 million they shelled out to Everton in 2000. Quite simply Dunne was one of the best defenders City have ever had.

Aged just 20. Dunne represented something of a gamble for manager Joe Royle and his early years at City suggested that gamble may not pay off. Though clearly talented, Dunne had a habit of shooting himself in the foot and was the subject of several breaches of club discipline, culminating in Kevin Keegan coming within an ace of sacking the player for one misdemeanour too many. Lurking beneath his jack-the-lad behaviour, however, was an unpolished diamond and Dunne finally got his act together off the pitch to stunning effect on it. Deceptively quick and very skilful for a defender. he soon became viewed as irreplaceable and one of the club's most important players.

Partnering Sylvian Distin, he was hailed as one of the best defenders in the Premiership, as important to City as John Terry was to Chelsea. Dunne was crowned Player of the Year for four successive seasons (2005-2008) and took over the captain's armband in 2003. In total he played 352 times for the club, scoring seven goals before joining Aston Villa in 2009 and later playing for QPR. He won 80 caps for the Republic of Ireland, scoring eight times. He holds the joint Premier League record for being sent off eight times - along with Patrick Vieira and Duncan Ferguson. He also holds the Premier League record of scoring 10 own goals.

EDERSON

Born in Osasco in Brazil on 17 August 1993, Ederson Santana de Moraes can lay claim to being as good a goalkeeper as any worldwide. The Premier League Golden Glove winner for three years running from 2019-20 he was also named in the PFA Premier League Team of the Year in 2020-21 and 2018-19, as well as the Champions League Squad of the Season in 2020-21.

Ederson's athleticism, agility, positional sense and wonderful distribution set the tone for City's astonishing quality right from the base of the goalkeeping position. Having cost a reported £35m in 2017 Ederson started as he meant to go on with a clean sheet at Brighton. To the end of 2022-23 the 6' 3" keeper had played 288+1 City games.

It was in 2008 that he started playing for Sao Paolo where he did so well that just a year later he earned a move to Europe to Benfica when he was still just 16. In 2011 he moved to Ribeirao gaining early experience with 29 league appearances. After a year in the second tier in Portuguese football the next step was up to the Primeira League with Rio Ave. Debuting at home to Maritimo on 18 August 2012 Ederson went on to play 39 times for the club before Benfica came back in for him in July 2015.

On 5 March 2016 he was thrust into the heat of a Lisbon derby, keeping a clean sheet away to Sporting on his Benfica debut. Four days later he played in a dramatic Champions League win at Zenit St. Petersburg, where two goals in the last five minutes gave Ederson's side victory.

In the next round he played both legs against Bayern Munich who edged the tie 3-2 on aggregate but he went on to help Benfica to a domestic double. Quickly establishing himself as the club's number one after being beaten once in his first match of 2016-17 - against Besiktas in the Champions League - he proceeded to keep six successive clean sheets. He ended the season with 21 shut-outs in 34 games before joining City after retaining the league and cup, as well as winning the Portuguese Supercup.

Since coming to City Ederson's quality has helped keep the silverware coming with five Premier League titles in his first six seasons. He also played in the 2019 FA Cup final as Watford were beaten 6-0 and the same year's League Cup final as Chelsea were beaten on penalties. At international level Ederson marked his debut for Brazil with a clean sheet against Chile in October 2017 and having been in Brazil's squad at the 2018 FIFA World Cup and the 2019 Copa America he was first choice and played in the 2021 Copa America final as Brazil lost 1-0 to Argentina. He won his 21st cap for his country against Senegal in June 2023.

ELANO

City's first Brazilian import came in the form of midfield playmaker Elano in the summer of 2007. The Blues paid approximately £8m to bring the Brazilian star from the Ukranian outfit Shakhtar Donetsk and he instantly became a crowd favourite with a series of virtuoso displays and spectacular goals throughout the first half of the campaign.

Successive 25-yard free kicks against Newcastle and Middlesbrough had the City fans eating out of Elano's hand, though he suffered a dip in form as the winter months kicked in and his effectiveness waned. As a tiring campaign, which included many long plane journeys for the Brazilian international, drew to a close, Elano began to rediscover the sparkle that had won him a legion of fans and he ended the season in fine form and finished as the club's top scorer with goals. Despite his popularity, he was allowed to join Galatasaray in July 2009.

ENGLAND

To the start of 2023-24, 52 players had been capped by England while with Manchester City. Goalkeeper Joe Hart was capped 64 times while with City. Raheem Sterling's appearance against Hungary at Wolverhampton Wanderers in the summer of 2022 was his 61st cap with City. Colin Bell won 48 while with the club, James Milner 42 and John Stones took his City tally to 57 by July 2023.

Other players to be capped with England while with City, in alphabetical order and with the number of caps won with City (Up to July 2023) in brackets, are: Sam Austin (1), Sam Barkas (5), Peter Barnes (14), Gareth Barry (24), Joey Barton (1), Frank Booth (1), Jackie Bray (6), Wayne Bridge (4), Ivor Broadis (8), Eric Brook (18), Herbert Burgess (4), Mick Channon (1), Joe Corrigan (9), Sam Cowan (3), Keith Curle (3), Fabian Delph (14), Mike Doyle (5), Phil Foden (25), Trevor Francis (10), Jack Grealish (20), David James (13), Adam Johnson (12), Tosh Johnson (2), Franny Lee (27), Joleon Lescott (19), Rodney Marsh (8), Jimmy Meadows (1), Jim Mitchell (1), Kalvin Phillips (4), Kevin Reeves (1), Don Revie (6), Micah Richards (13), Frank Roberts (4), Jack Rodwell (1), Joe Royle (4), Trevor Sinclair (1), Bert Sproston (1), Mike Summerbee (8), Frank Swift (19), Irvine Thornley (1), Fred Tilson (4), Dennis Tueart (6), Kyle Walker (49), Dave Watson (27), David White (1), Max Woosnam (1) and Shaun Wright-Phillips (20).

JOE HART AND JOHN STONES IN ENGLAND ACTION

ETIHAD

City moved into their state of the art stadium in time for the start of the 2003-04 season. Christened the 'City of Manchester' stadium, it is widely regarded as one of the best in Britain and Europe and in 2008 hosted the UEFA Cup Final between Rangers and Zenit St Petersburg. Housing 48,000 supporters, the futuristic stadium was originally home to the hugely successful 2002 Commonwealth Games held in the city.

Many believed that the stadium should remain an athletics arena but without City's commitment and financial backing, the venue would have been a temporary sporting arena built and then dismantled afterwards. Once the Games had finished, the running track was dug up and the playing surface lowered by several metres to uncover the lower tiers of each stand, which had been buried under tons of soil.

There was one temporary stand in the stadium that was completed in time for the Blues to take up permanent residency following 80 years at Maine Road. City opened the stadium by beating Barcelona 2-1 while the first competitive game was a UEFA Cup qualifier against Total Network Solutions that the Blues won 5-0. In 2011 the stadium naming rights were purchased by Etihad Airways and ever since City's home has been known as 'The Etihad'.

In 2015 City's success meant the stadium had to be extended with a third tier on the South Stand. It now has a capacity of 55,017. In 2015 over 50,000 attended a rugby international between England and Uruguay while the following year just under 45,000 saw England (who had previously played two friendlies at the stadium against Japan and Iceland) beat Turkey with Jamie Vardy and Harry Kane scoring in a 2-1 warm up win for Euro 2016.

EUROPEAN CUP-WINNERS' CUP

A now defunct tournament of Europe's domestic cup-winning sides was one that Manchester City mastered and almost successfully defended. The 1969 FA Cup Final victory over Leicester City had given Joe Mercer's side a fast-track back into Europe following the European Cup disappointment 12 months earlier.

In what would prove to be an exciting adventure on the continent, the Blues put on a terrific display of gutsy, attacking football to eliminate Atletico Bilbao, SK Lierse, Academia Coimbra and Schalke 04 before goals from Franny lee and Neil Young helped City beat Polish side Gornik Zabrze in the final, played in atrocious conditions in the Prater Stadium, Vienna. City and their first European trophy and for many years their only major European trophy until they won the Champions League in 2023.

Only an injury crisis at a critical stage of their defence of the trophy denied City the chance of a second successive final after successfully seeing off the challenges of Linfield, Honved and Gornik Zabrze to reach the semi-finals where Chelsea triumphed over two legs, winning each 1-0. With a fit and full squad, Mercer's side may well have gone on to win the Cup-Winners' Cup again.

TONY BOOK IS PRESENTED WITH THE EUROPEAN CUP WINNERS' CUP AFTER HIS TEAM'S 2-1 VICTORY OVER GORNIK ZABRZE, 29 APRIL 1970

FA CUP

Seven times winners of the world's oldest football competition, most recently defeating near neighbours Manchester United in the 2023 final, City first entered in 1890-91 when the club were called Ardwick and beat Liverpool Stanley 12-0 in their first game.

As Manchester City on the other hand the first game in the FA Cup (Or English Cup as it was known then) was lost 6-0 to Preston North End on 30 January 1897. The first time the Blues lifted the trophy was in 1904 with a narrow 1-0 win over Bolton at The Crystal Palace; the same season they missed out on a historic league and cup double after finishing runners-up in Division One.

Bolton would have their revenge in 1926, winning the cup by scoring the game's only goal in City's first ever Wembley appearance. Seven years after that, City were again on the losing side, this time to Everton by a crushing score line of 3-0. Captain Sam Cowan vowed to return with his side the following year and lift the trophy as winners and he was true to his word as the Blues beat Portsmouth 2-1 in the 1934 final.

History repeated itself in 1955 when City went down 3-1 to Newcastle United only to go all the way the next year and win the competition 3-1 over Birmingham City. It would be 1969 before the Blues tasted more success in the world's most famous club competition - a Neil Young thunderbolt giving Joe Mercer's side in a 1-0 victory over Leicester. In 1981 Tommy Hutchison scored for both sides in a 1-1 draw with Tottenham before Spurs won the replay 3-2 with a famous goal from Argentinian Ricky Villa.

Thirty years later, in 2011 a Yaya Toure goal secured the trophy with a 1-0 final victory over Stoke City. Two years after that City were on the wrong end of a 1-0 cup final scoreline when Wigan scored a stoppage time winner through Ben Watson in what was a huge upset, City having been reduced to ten men when Pablo Zabaleta was dismissed.

In 2019 City equalled the record FA Cup final score of 6-0 (held by Bury who beat Derby in 1903). David Silva and Gabriel Jesus had City two to the good at half time after which Kevin De Bruyne and Jesus again doubled the lead, before two late goals from Raheem Sterling completed the rout. City were finalists again in 2021 but in a reversal of the scoreline from 1969 this time it was Leicester City's turn to win 1-0 with a spectacular goal from Youri Tielemans.

FERNANDINHO

Best at the base of midfield where he could dictate play, snuff out danger and start attacks, Fernandinho was also noted for his long range shots. Joining City in 2013, he cost a reported £34m from Shakhtar Donetsk where he won six Ukrainian league titles, four domestic cups, the Ukrainian Supercup and the UEFA Cup. He was one of five Brazilians in the side as Shakhtar beat Werder Bremen in the 2009 final.

A FIFA World Youth Championship winner with Brazil in 2019 he won the Copa America with his national team in 2019 and to 2021 has over 50 caps. His trophy cabinet has kept bulging since coming to England. The 2020-21 Premier League title was Fernandinho's fourth, to which he can add winner's medals from six League Cup finals including 2016 when he scored and 2021 when he was captain. In the summer of 2022 he returned to Brazil with Paranaense after 321+62 games for the club, in which he scored 26 times.

FLOODLIGHTS

'Let There be light' - and there was - with midweek evening games becoming an atmospheric new addition to the English league season. Four towering floodlights were erected at Maine Road in 1953 and the inaugural floodlit match was a friendly against Hearts on October 14th that same year. The Blues wore special 'shiny shirts' for the evening and won an entertaining game 6-3 in front of almost 24,000 curious fans.

The innovative lighting brought Manchester United back to Maine Road (they had ground shared with City during the Second World War) to play various friendlies and cup games until Old Trafford had their own floodlights installed in 1957. Not, however, before Maine Road became the first English ground to play host to a European Cup match in 1956 – though sadly the Blues weren't even involved as United beat RSC Anderlecht 10-0.

FODEN

Born on 28 May 2000, Phil Foden is the future
of football for Manchester City and England. In the
decade to come he is likely to be as bright a star as
any in the game. The Golden Ball winner as he helped
England win the FIFA Under 17 World Cup in 2017
he went on to become the youngest man to win the
Premier League and the youngest UEFA Champions
League scorer. Phil's flair balance and pace make him
one of the most exciting players to emerge in England
in recent decades.

Probably best as an out and out left winger, in the
modern game players need to be versatile enough to
play in different positions, often within the same match,
especially for coaches as tactically astute as Pep Guardiola
and Gareth Southgate. Foden has risen to all challenges,
illustrating that he has a football brain to match his
precocious talent with the ball at his feet.

With winners medals numbered in double-figures by the
age of 21 and having won the Champions League, five
Premier League titles and six domestic cups by the age of
23 goodness knows how big a trophy cabinet Foden will
need by the time he hangs up his boots!

FOE

Few could have realised the long-lasting impression Marc Vivien Foe would leave on Manchester City fans following his season-long loan from French side Lyon. A holding midfielder, the tall Cameroonian was signed by Kevin Keegan to add steel to a creative midfield that included Eyal Berkovic, Ali Benarbia and Shaun Wright-Philips and though initially he wasn't appreciated by the majority of City fans, it soon became clear that he was doing a fantastic job for the team, not too dissimilar to the role Patrick Vieira had done so effectively for Arsenal for several years.

Foe then added several vital goals to the City cause, with his telescopic legs connecting to several half-chances and his popularity soared.

During the penultimate game to be played at Maine Road, City took on Sunderland and it was Foe who scored what turned out to be the last goal by a City player at the famous old stadium in a 3-0 win.

At the end of the 2002-03 season, Keegan began negotiations to bring Foe to City on a permanent basis but during a Confederations Cup match for Cameroon against Columbia in June 2003, he slumped to the ground having suffered a massive and fatal heart attack. He was just 28 years-old. The shock waves were felt throughout the sporting world and the old Maine Road became a shrine of flowers, shirts and scarves from all around the world as fans paid their respects to this most gentle, popular man.

FOOTBALL LEAGUE CUP

Four successive League Cup triumphs from 2017 to 2021 brought City level with Liverpool as the leading League Cup winners with eight wins each. The competition began in 1960-61 with Stockport County City's first opponents, City winning 3-0. City first appeared in the fourth Wembley final, beating WBA in 1970. Four years later they lost 2-1 in the final to Wolves but returned two years later to beat Newcastle United 2-1 with probably the best goal ever seen in a League Cup final - Dennis Tueart's bicycle-kick against his home team.

It was Tueart's old club Sunderland who were defeated in City's next League Cup final which didn't come until 2014 but since then City have dominated the competition. It took penalties to beat Liverpool in 2016 and Chelsea in 2019 but in between Arsenal were put to the sword to the tune of 3-0 in 2018. Aston Villa were then defeated 2-1 in 2020 with a late goal from Aymeric Laporte sealing a 1-0 victory over Tottenham Hotspur in 2021.

THE TEAM POSE WITH THE CARABAO CUP AFTER THEIR 2-1 WIN OVER SPURS, APRIL 2021

FRANCIS

More than 10,000 City fans travelled to Stoke to watch Trevor Francis make his debut for the Blues after the much-coveted striker joined the club in 1981 for £1.2 million. The England man did not disappoint, either, scoring twice in a 3-2 win. Francis positively oozed class and he was graceful and electrifying to watch.

His stay at Maine Road, however, was blighted by injury, though he inspired City to the top of the table over the 1981 festive period following a 3-1 Boxing Day victory at Liverpool and a 2-1 win against Wolves two days later. He only managed 29 appearances for the Blues but scored 14 goals including several fantastic individual efforts.

An intelligent forward, he would bring others into the game and inspired those around him, especially the younger forwards, to reach greater heights but the stop/start nature of his time at the club proved frustrating to everyone, not least the player.

He reluctantly joined Italian Serie A club Sampdoria for approximately £1 million having played for just one season at Maine Road - the truth was the cash-strapped Blues could no longer afford to keep their prize asset, though the impression he left behind was huge. The football world was shocked when he died of a heart attack at his home in Marbella, Spain, on July 24, 2023, aged 69.

FULL MEMBERS CUP

This much-maligned competition was sponsored by several obscure companies during its relatively brief existence. The Simod Cup, Zenith Data Systems ...call it what you will, but it was the plain old Full Members' Cup in 1985-86 when City tentatively entered and it would be the one and only time the trophy registered in the hearts and minds of Blues supporters.

With English clubs banned from European competition, the FMC hoped to become the third major cup competition in England but it was always destined to fail due to its lack of prestige and no real incentive to win the trophy. Considered as little more than a joke by most of the football world, both City and Chelsea progressed through sparse crowds until they met at Wembley. Despite the general apathy surrounding the competition, some 68,000 fans turned out on the day and enjoyed a quite spectacular feast of attacking football that ebbed and flowed in the dramatic traditions befitting both clubs. City went ahead through Mark Lillis but the Pensioners roared back with a vengeance to lead 5-1 with just minutes left.

Incredibly, City pulled back three goals through Lillis, Kinset and an own-goal, and almost scrambled an equaliser, ultimately losing 5-4. The Blues never again reached such dizzy heights in the competition and their last appearance was in 1991-92. The competition ceased completely a couple of years later.

GOATER

Shaun Goater - or 'The GOAT' as he became known and loved - managed to turn jeers of derision into flat-out hero worship over a six-year period at Maine Road. Signed by Joe Royle for a bargain £400,000 from Bristol City, few regarded him as little more than a stop-gap - a journeyman striker whose goals might save the club from relegation to the Third Division in 1997-98. His four goals in nine starts weren't enough and he found himself playing for a side who had been replaced in a higher division by his old side Bristol City.

Goater's unorthodox style certainly got results but it would be almost two years before the fans realised that his hard work and honest style were actually a refreshing change to many of the game's over pampered stars and an appreciation quickly grew with the terraces. It was also the first time in many years that the Blues had an instinctive striker who could bring in 20 to 30 goals each season without fail. Shaun's goals steered City out of Division Two in 1999 and his 29 goals the following campaign ensured a second successive promotion for the Blues.

Injury beset the Bermudian international during the doomed 2000-01 Premiership campaign but he still finished the season in red-hot form with seven in his last nine games, proving he could score goals at any level, and his 32 goals in the 2001-02 season enabled the Blues to win promotion back to the Premiership at the first attempt. In his final season, he scored his 100th goal for the club in the historic final Manchester derby at Maine Road and his anthem 'Feed the Goat and he will score' became one of the most famous chants in football.

GREALISH

Britain's first £100m footballer when City bought the England creator from Aston Villa in August 2021, Grealish was the man Guardiola believed guaranteed the quality required to make sure the champions kept on improving.

Born on 10 September 1995 in Birmingham, Jack joined Villa when he was only six but made his senior debut on loan to Notts County four days after turning 18. Coming off the bench for Notts in a 3-1 defeat at MK Dons, on a day when Chelsea loanee Patrick Bamford scored for the Dons, few if any of the 7,142 crowd might have imagined that the sub with his socks distinctively half way down his calves would go on to become the UK's first £100m player.

By the end of the season Meadow Lane regulars might have begun to contemplate such a stellar future for Grealish who showed his class by beating three defenders as he scored his first goal against Gillingham and ended the season with five goals and seven assists. Villa were certainly impressed and immediately following his loan handed Jack a Premier League debut on the penultimate day of the season as a late substitute in a 4-0 defeat - at Manchester City.

The following season ended for him in another 4-0 defeat - but this time in the FA Cup final to Arsenal after he had provided the assist for Fabian Delph's winner in the semi-final against Liverpool. Another 4-0 defeat to the Gunners in Grealish's last game of the next 2015-16 campaign was even more disastrous as Villa were relegated, with Jack on the losing side in all 16 of his Premier League appearances.

He then endured three years in the Championship before Play-Off joy against Derby in 2019, a year after he had played in a Play-Off final defeat to Fulham. Approaching his 24th birthday by the time he re-emerged in the Premier League, Jack was now at a stage where he could dominate rather than decorate top-flight matches. Adhesive control, a super-car style change of pace and the ability to pick a pass whilst gliding over the turf at speed marked him out as a real star. He was Villa Players' Player of the Season and Supporters' Player of the Season in 2019-20 during which he was also the Premier League's most fouled player

With three Irish grandparents Jack was well qualified to play for the Republic of Ireland which he did 19 times at Under 17, 18 and 21 levels, being the Republic's Under 17 Player of the Year in 2012 and Under 21 Player of the Year two years later. However Grealish's great-great grandad

Billy Garraty, played for England. Capped against Wales in 1903 he played over 200 games for Villa with whom he twice won the league as well as the FA Cup and was the Football League's top-scorer in 1899-1900. On 28 September 2015 Jack announced his decision to switch his international allegiance to England and in May of the following year made his bow at Under 21 level. After debuting as a sub against Portugal he scored twice on his full debut against Guinea at the Toulon Tournament.

He won seven England Under 21 caps before making his full debut as a sub in a goalless draw away to Denmark in September 2020. Nine months later he again appeared as a sub against the Danes, but this time in the semi-final of the delayed Euro 2020 tournament in which he also came off the bench in the final against Italy. That was his 12th cap won with Villa. To July 2023 Grealish had added another 20 while on City's books, scoring his first international goals against Andorra and Iran.

MAINE ROAD

RIGHT:
THE ETIHAD STADIUM

GROUNDS

Encompassing all the names City have played under,
the following is a list of the grounds that the club has,
at some point or other, called home:

1880-81	CLOWES STREET
1881-82	KIRKMANSHULME LANE CRICKET CLUB
1882-84	QUEENS ROAD
1884-85	PINK BANK LANE
1885-87	THE BULL'S HEAD HOTEL, REDDISH LANE
1887-1923	HYDE ROAD
1923-2003	MAINE ROAD
2003-PRESENT	ETIHAD STADIUM

PEP WITH HIS HANDS ON THE
PREMIER LEAGUE TROPHY, MAY 2021

GUARDIOLA

The most successful manager in the club's history Pep Guardiola quickly became a legend at City. Born on 18 January 1971 in Santpedor in the Catalan region of Spain, Josep Guardiola Sala was a legend long before he became a manager. At Barcelona he played under the great Johan Cruyff, winning the European Cup (now the Champions League) in 1992, anchoring the midfield in the final as a Sampdoria side including Roberto Mancini and Gianluca Vialli were beaten at Wembley.

Five years later he also won the Cup Winners' Cup under the guidance of Bobby Robson as Barca beat PSG in Rotterdam. With six La Liga titles, four Spanish Supercups, two European Supercups and the Copa del Rey, plus 47 Spain caps, as well as seven representative appearances for Catalonia, Pep's personal trophy cabinet was overflowing before he moved into management.

Tactically innovative, Guardiola's sides haven't just been serial trophy winners, they have redefined so many aspects of accepted football wisdom. Full-backs popping up in central midfield, midfielders being utilised in central defence and the most successful attacking team in football sometimes taking to the field without a recognised centre-forward are just three of the revelations he has brought to the British game.

Side-lining England goalkeeper Joe Hart immediately upon his arrival at City signalled that Pep wanted players who could play - starting with the keeper. Pep's teams dominate possession and press to get the ball back quickly when it is lost. Always ultra-professional, Pep's preparation means that his team do not take to the pitch without a deep understanding of the strength's and weaknesses of their opponents.

Before coming to City Guardiola twice won both the Champions League and European Super Cup with Barcelona who he also led to three successive La Liga's from 2009 to 2011. In each of those seasons Pep also triumphed in the Spanish Supercup, as well as twice winning the Copa del Rey and twice triumphing in the FIFA Club World Cup.

Having moved to Bayern Munich Guardiola repeated the feat of winning his domestic title three years in a row - from 2014 to 2016. He also twice won the German Cup, the DFB-Pokal, and won both the UEFA Super Cup and FIFA Club World Cup upon his arrival in 2013.

At City the silverware has kept coming. Achieving the treble of Premier League, FA Cup and a first ever Champions League triumph was the pinnacle of his time so far. The 2022-23 Premier League title was the fifth such success in six seasons with six domestic cups won during the same period.

Three times League Managers' Association Manager of the Year and eleven times Manager of the Month, Pep was named La Liga Coach of the Year in every year from 2009 to 2012, and in 2009 and 2011 won European coach of the Year awards. To the end of the 2022-23 season Guardiola had guided City to 197 wins in 266 Premier League matches, a win percentage of 74%.

City have had many great teams and many great managers, but surely there can be no dispute that the era under Pep Guardiola is the best of all. The great thing for City fans is that going into 2023-24 the golden age is still in full flow.

GUNDOGAN

Born in Gelsenkirchen in Germany on 24 October 1990, Ilkay Gundogan was Pep Guardiola's first signing for City, the reported fee of £20m a bargain for a deceptively quick technician of the highest standard. Gundogan's stature as a key player for City is illustrated by him playing a minimum of 46 games in each season from 2017-18 to 2022-23 - reaching 62 appearances for club and country in his final City season where he signed off with both goals as Manchester United were beaten in the FA Cup final before he lifted the Champions League a week later.

2020-21 saw him score a personal best of 17 goals, making him City's top scorer in a season in which he scored a further four times for Germany. The fluidity of Guardiola's system made Gundogan's creativity and goalscoring ever more influential, particularly when the team operate with a 'false 9.' When injury meant City had to play without the talismanic Kevin De Bruyne, Gundogan came more and more to the fore.

Prior to coming to City the Germany international had spent five years with Borussia Dortmund for whom he scored with a penalty at Wembley in 2013 in an all-German Champions League final lost 2-1 to Bayern Munich. The previous year he had done the domestic double with Dortmund.

Ilkay had come to prominence with FC Nurnberg, making his Bundesliga debut at Werder Bremen in March 2010. After 60 goals in 234+70 games for City Ilkay moved on to Barcelona at the age of 32 in the summer of 2023.

HAALAND

Re-write the record books! A sensational sixty one goals in his first season included nine for Norway and a phenomenal 52 for City including a record 36 in the Premier League. Successive Premier League hat-tricks against Palace and Forest came as part of an incredible run of scoring in 11 successive City games, netting an amazing total of 19 goals in that run.

A third hat-trick came as local rivals Manchester United were walloped 6-3 with a fourth match ball making its way to Haaland's home after another treble against Wolves. Soon afterwards Erling smashed five in a 7-0 Champions League thrashing of RB Leipzig and five days later bagged an FA Cup hat-trick as Vincent Kompany's Burnley were beaten 6-0. Helping City to the treble of Champions League, Premier League and FA Cup in his first season in Manchester was surely beyond even the wildest dreams of himself or the City fans excited when he signed from Borussia Dortmund for £51.2m on 13 June 2022.

In Germany Erling had scored 62 Bundesliga goals in 59 starts plus eight games as a sub and a total of 86 goals in 79+10 games in total. Dortmund had paid £18m, to buy him from Red Bull Salzburg on New Year's Day 2020. In Austria the goal machine had scored a total of 25 times in only 16 +7 appearances. Salzburg more than doubled their outlay, having paid £7m to Norwegian outfit Molde exactly a year earlier. Haaland had made his name in his own country with 14 goals in 20+19 matches after not scoring in the 4+12 games he had with Bryne as a youth.

Aged just 16 when he debuted for Molde in the Norwegian Tippeligaen in June 2017, Erling was under three weeks passed his 17th birthday when he scored his first senior goal at Tromso. Still 17 when he scored all four in 4-0 win at Brann, the teenager was already attracting attention from around the continent.

Eight goals in six games preceded his full international debut against Malta in September 2019. Returning to Salzburg after the international break hat-tricks in consecutive games, including one in the Champions League against Genk of Belgium, underlined his credentials. After yet another three-goal haul he moved to Germany where a debut hat-trick for Dortmund at Augsburg signalled 11 goals in his first seven games.

The son of former City player Alfie Haaland, Erling Braut Haaland was born in Leeds, who his father was playing for at the time, on 21 July 2000. A league and cup winner with Red Bull Salzburg, Erling also won the DFB-Pokal with Dortmund before doubling his senior trophy haul in his first year with City. Footballer of the Year, European Golden Shoe winner, Premier League Player and Young Player of the Season and of course City Player of the Season were just some of the individual awards the superstar won in 2022-23.

Physically powerful, tall, fast and determined, Haaland smashed record after record in his first year in English football. In the years to come he could blast every record going and if that proves to be the case the continued success City could have is mind-boggling.

HAALAND BECAME THE FASTEST PLAYER IN PREMIER LEAGUE HISTORY TO REACH 50 GOALS, NETTING HIS 50TH AGAINST LIVERPOOL IN HIS 48TH GAME, 25 NOVEMBER 2023

HART

Having won **64** of his **75** England caps while with City, with the other **11** all coming while he was on loan from the club, to the start of the **2021-22** season Hart remains the player to have made most appearances for England whilst a Manchester City player. Add to this **19** internationals as an unused sub for England while with City and the fact that he twice captained the national side and it is evident that as a goalkeeper Joe Hart spent a long time at the top of the tree. As a four time Premier League Golden Glove winner between **2011** and **2015** that is not in doubt. To **2023** he remains the only Englishman to win the award that no keeper has won more often.

A commanding, physically imposing and confident 'keeper, Hart twice won the Premier League and League Cup with City as well as playing in two FA Cup finals, keeping a clean sheet as Stoke were beaten in 2011 and only conceding an injury-time goal in defeat to Wigan two years later.

However following the appointment of Pep Guardiola Hart was allowed to move on with the coach evidently preferring a goalkeeper he felt was more comfortable with the ball at his feet.

Subsequently following loans to Torino and West Ham Hart transferred to Burnley where after 24 appearances over two years he moved on to Tottenham in 2020 making ten appearances for them - all in cup games in 2020-21. In 2021 Joe moved to Celtic where by 2023 he had added to his trophy haul with back-to-back league titles and three domestic cups.

Born in Shrewsbury on 19 April 1987 Joe started with 58 games for his hometown team before coming to City in May 2006 and building up his experience with loans to Tranmere Rovers, Blackpool and Birmingham City (where he was Player of the Year) in his early years at the club. A Premier League debut with City came before any of those loans, Joe keeping a clean sheet against Sheffield United in October 2006. He went on to play a total of 348 times for City, 266 of those in the Premier League and earned his place in the hearts of City supporters.

HARTFORD

Scottish international Asa Hartford must have had one of the most famous medicals in the history of football after a hole was discovered in his heart on the eve of a move from West Brom to Leeds United. Crestfallen, Hartford continued to ply his trade at the Hawthorns before City boss Tony Book made an offer for his services and after a stringent medical he was given the green light by the club doctor who said that the condition should have no bearing whatsoever on his football career.

A busy, all-action midfielder, Hartford was signed from WBA in 1974 for a fee of £250,000 and he soon became the beating heart of the 1970s team. Asa went on to win 36 caps for his country while at Maine Road - a record number of Scottish caps for a City player - and formed an excellent partnership with Gary Owen and Peter Barnes.

He was the driving force behind the Blues' bid to lift the League title in 1976-77 when they agonisingly missed out by a point to Liverpool. He was sold by Malcolm Allison in 1979 to Nottingham Forest for £500,000 but returned to City two years later making another 88 appearances before jetting off for the North American Soccer League.

He returned to the club for a third spell in 1993 to assist Alan Ball after management spells at Shrewsbury and Stockport and later took charge of the reserves until 2006, before spending a final season in football as assistant manager at Macclesfield Town.

HUTCHISON

Tommy Hutchison time as a Manchester City player was relatively brief in the grand scheme of things and his 57 starts bear testament to that. But the stylish Scottish winger oozed class and left a long-lasting impression on those Blues fans that were fortunate enough to see him play. He joined City from Coventry for just £47,000 and formed part of John Bond's famous 'tartan trio' that also included Gerry Gow and Bobby McDonald. Together, they helped transform an ailing City side into a team that almost won the 1981 FA Cup.

Hutchison possessed excellent control and vision and a will to play football the way it was meant to be played. Due to his unfortunate and unique record, Tommy has the dubious privilege of appearing on a Trivial Pursuit question card. The question is: who is the only player to score for both sides in an FA Cup Final? Of course, the answer is Tommy Hutchison who scored with a flying header for City in the first half then deflected home a Spurs' free kick after eavesdropping on Glenn Hoddle's plans.

HYDE ROAD

SHAY STADIUM'S SKIRCOAT STAND (RIGHT) ONCE OF HYDE ROAD

Now the site of a Manchester bus company, Hyde Road was City's first enclosed ground and was home to Ardwick FC from 1887 to 1894 and then Manchester City FC from 1894 until 1923. Hemmed in by a railway track to the west and north sidings - train drivers would often slow down to catch a glimpse of City in action, presumably giving a toot of their whistle if things appeared to be going well! Crowds were only estimated at the time and ranged from as low as 500 up to 40,000.

The Blues were Division One runners-up on two occasions while at the ground but with the team's popularity growing at a phenomenal rate, it became clear that a new home was desperately needed.

Even more so after the main stand burned down in 1920. Belle Vue, a few miles up the road, was cited as a possible home but the eight-acre plot was not nearly enough to house the club.

Suitable land was found in Moss Side, several miles away, and the foundations of a new stadium were soon visible to curious supporters. In the summer of 1923, Maine Road was completed and City closed the gates at Hyde Road for the last time. One of the Hyde Road stands was sold to Halifax Town for the princely sum of £1000 and was still standing when the Blues lost 1-0 at The Shay in 1980. Today, the area the pitch once covered is now a skid pan for learner bus drivers!

MARTIN O'NEILL

BELOW:
NIALL QUINN

IRELAND

Peter Doherty, Johnny Crossan, Jeff and Jim Whitley, Steve Lomas, Michael Hughes, Sammy McIlroy and Martin O'Neill are amongst those who have worn the green of Northern Ireland as well as starring for Manchester City.

Niall Quinn, Mick McCarthy, Richard Dunne, Shay Given and of course Stephen Ireland have represented the Republic of Ireland whilst with City. Mickey Hammill played 118 league games for City in the early 1920s and won seven caps for Ireland before the complicated matter of the Republic and Northern Ireland came about.

JOHNSTONE

Bobby Johnstone earned the nickname 'Bobby Dazzler' for his exceptional skill on the ball. Born in Selkirk, the Scottish international arrived at Maine Road in March 1955 from Hibernian for a fee of £20,700. He made a sensational start to his Scotland career when he scored against England at Wembley, establishing him as one of the hottest properties of his generation.

He quickly became a popular figure on the terraces too with his attacking instincts and ability striking the right chords with the Blues' supporters. He made his debut against Bolton Wanderers and quickly made his way into the history books, when he became the first player ever to score in consecutive FA Cup Finals in 1955 and 1956

In all, he played 138 times for City, winning four of his 17 Scotland caps while at Maine Road, and rifled in 50 goals before he was transferred back to Hibs for £7,000 in 1959. He was also a keen cricketer and crown green bowler and finished his career playing for Oldham Athletic. Bobby died in 2001, aged 71.

KEEGAN

Few managers can lay claim to such an electrifying first season as the one enjoyed by Kevin Keegan in 2001-02. The former England legend was installed at Maine Road following Joe Royle's surprise sacking in May 2001 and his first signings were Stuart Pearce and Eyal Berkovic.

His first game in charge against Watford was a fantastic occasion, as the City fans packed Maine Road hoping to be entertained by the man who made Newcastle United into one of the most attractive team of the 1990s and went home delighted by what they had seen. 'The Keegan Factor' as it became known, encouraged open, attacking football and when he added Algerian midfielder Ali Benarbia into the mix, the football became a sublime fusion of devastating offensive play and something close to exhibition football. The fans lapped it up and City won the First Division at a canter, breaking a host of records along the way, not least goals scored which totalled 108 in the league alone.

As The Blues rolled back into the Premiership, so a galaxy of expensive talents was assembled at Maine Road, including the likes of Nicolas Anelka, Sylvian Distin and Peter Schmeichel. The Blues finished ninth in the Premiership and qualified for Europe via the Fair Play league. Nothing, it seemed, could go wrong. More big names arrived in the form of David Seaman, Robbie Fowler and Steve McManaman but the team had lost much of its zip and invention with Benarbia and Berkovic gone and not adequately replaced. A brush with relegation during the Blues first season at the City of Manchester stadium in 2003-04 and a disappointing 2004-05 campaign saw Keegan quit City, seemingly having lost the ability to motivate his players. Stuart Pearce, Keegan's recently appointed coach took the reins and the man they called 'Mighty Mouse' disappeared into the ether. For the first two years, however, Keegan was simply 'King Kev' to his goal-hungry City fans.

KIDD

Despite a fairly slow start in front of goal, it didn't take too long for Brian Kidd top ease the memory of his heroics for Manchester United following a £110,000 buy from Arsenal in 1976. 'Kiddo' would play a large part in City's successful mid-1970s team and seemed to enjoy ruffling the feathers of one or two former teammates during the Manchester derby games.

He took ten games in the league to find the net for City and by the end of November he'd managed just one strike in 13 games. But if there were any doubters, they were well and truly silenced as Kidd suddenly hit form - and then some. He scored ten goals in his next seven outings and struck four times in a 5-0 win over Leicester City, finishing the season with 21 goals from 39 games - his efforts had almost helped bring home the championship in his first season.

Kiddo went on to total 56 goals in 127 starts plus one appearance as a sub in three years as a City player but had even greater success as part of the backroom staff which he left in July 2021 after 12 years. City won 16 trophies under three managers while Brian offered his support. Initially brought in to help develop youngsters he became an exceptionally highly valued assistant to Roberto Mancini, Manuel Pellegrini and Pep Guardiola.

KINKLADZE

Little was known of 21-year-old midfielder Georgi Kinkladze when he signed for City shortly before the start of the 1995-96 campaign. New manager Alan Ball took just one training session to claim that the Georgian would have the City fans "hanging from the rafters to watch him play".

Not long into his debut on a hot, sunny August afternoon, it was clear to all in attendance that Kinkladze had the kind of individual skill rarely - if ever - seen at Maine Road before. Within a few months he was idolised by the fans and heralded by the pundits and the national media. He was a precocious talent, someone who got people out of their seats with his incredible dribbles and incisive precision passing. He made goals, scored them and invariably there would be at least two or three moments in a game when he could take your breath away.

Each goal he scored for the club was memorable and the solo effort against Southampton when he beat five players before chipping the ball impudently past Dave Beasant is regarded by most as one of the best ever goals by a City player. 'Kinky', as the fans were calling him by now, couldn't stop the Blues escaping relegation when a 2-2 draw with Liverpool was not enough to prevent City returning to Division One.

It wasn't long before Liverpool and Barcelona were linked with a £10m swoop for the player while Sir Alex Ferguson, off record, is alleged that the only player at that time he would have signed was Kinkladze but he knew that City would never sell their prized asset to their deadliest rivals.

Gio stayed to try and help the Blues bounce back at the first attempt, sparkling here and there and scoring a dozen league goals along the way. City finished a disastrous 14th but following an amazing show of support for the Georgian in the final game of the season at home to Reading, he decided to give it one last shot.

His final year was not a happy one. He looked frustrated and disappointed as City headed towards Division Two. Frank Clark had taken over from Ball and Joe Royle took over from Clark as the managerial merry-go-round continued at the club. Royle was bemused by what he felt was an unhealthy obsession with Kinky at the club and sold him to Ajax not long after arriving. The love affair between City fans and Kinky was over but the memories of this most gifted player still linger to this day.

KIPPAX

Home to thousands upon thousands of City fans from 1923 to the closure of Maine Road, this famous much-loved old terrace was often the extra man for the Blues as the supporters roared their heroes on to success.

It was over 35 years before a roof was erected to keep the Manchester rain off the supporters' heads and, with a smart new covering, the side of the ground generally known as the 'popular side' was officially named the Kippax Stand. It was home to 32,000 fans, though this was reduced to 26,155 when the North Stand was completed in 1971. Further reductions meant that only 18,300 City fans stood in the cavernous old stand near its lamentable demise.

The Taylor Report, a government-backed investigation into the safety of standing areas at football grounds, recommended that all terracing become seated areas, effectively signalling the end for the Kippax as a terraced stand. City supporters paid their final respects to their favourite part of the ground on 30 April 1994 when City took on Chelsea. Fancy dress, flags and balloons festooned the Kippax celebrating its 71-year life. Many shed a tear after the final whistle and attempted to chip bits of concrete off steps as a souvenir.

The new Kippax stand was opened to City fans for the first home game of the 1995-96 season and many fans groaned as they took their seats in the second and top tiers on first inspection - nothing to do with the perfect view of the pitch but because Old Trafford was now visible in the distance!

KOMPANY

Over 11 seasons in which he captained the club in eight campaigns, Vincent started 338 games and came off the bench another 22 times, scoring 20 goals. He won four Premier League titles, two Community Shields, the FA Cup twice and the League Cup four times, making many notable contributions. One of the most telling was a razor sharp, inch perfect tackle on Fabio Borini, who was clean through looking to double Sunderland's lead he had already given them in the 2014 League (Capital One) Cup final. City went on to take the trophy and while goalscorers tend to take the headlines, so often Kompany was the key man.

Player of the Year at City in 2010-11 he was named in the PFA Team of the Year three times and collected the Goal of the Season gong in 2019. This was for a real captain's goal - a screamer from outside the box that decided a key fixture with Leicester City. Leaving that indelible memory of a great goal to add to all his defensive and organisational attributes, Vincent left at the end of that season.

While City had signed Kompany from Hamburg he had started with Anderlecht who he returned to as player/head coach. Throughout his time in England he remained a regular in the Belgium international team, playing 89 times for his country. Beginning his managerial career with Anderlecht he took them to the Belgian cup final in 2022 before taking over at Burnley who he led to the Championship with a magnificent 101 points in his first season of 2022-23.

LAW

Though Denis Law spent the best years of his career at Old Trafford, he had enough memorable games in a City shirt - over two spells separated by a decade - to be forgiven for his efforts elsewhere. One of the game's most instinctive strikers, he once famously scored a double hat-trick against Luton, only for the game to be abandoned due to the torrential rain creating a surface more suitable for boating than football. Typically, City lost the re-match 3-1 and Law had to be content with just a consolation goal.

Joining City from Huddersfield Town, a scrawny teenage Law scored 23 times in his first season at Maine Road (29 times if you throw in the abandoned match) before Italian giants Torino made a British record offer of £125,000 which City accepted. As time went on, the talented Scot found a way to what would become his spiritual home with the Reds before returning to Maine Road for one last hurrah, having been released by United.

Even in the twilight of his career, Law scored important goals for the Blues and featured in a dream - though ageing - forward line of March, Summerbee and Lee. His final kick in league football was the impish back heel that confirmed his former club United's relegation to Division Two. How they must have regretted allowing such a lethal talent to join their deadly rivals.

Sadly, in August 2021 Dennis issued a statement announcing he was suffering from dementia.

LEE

A player who can truly be called a Manchester City legend, Francis Lee signed for City in 1967 aged 23, and was destined to become one of Joe Mercer's most influential signings. The Blues paid £60,000 for the stocky forward's services and for many, he was the final piece in the jigsaw that Mercer and Malcolm Allison had put together. A lethal finisher, with a cannonball shot, Franny was also the most prolific penalty taker the club had ever known with many arguing he won spot kicks unfairly. His 13 penalties in one season is easily a club record and he earned the nickname "Lee One Pen".

He averaged just under a goal every game for City and was an integral member of City's glory days, forging a fantastic understanding with Mike Summerbee and Colin Bell, dubbed 'The Holy Trinity'. A feisty so and so in a team of so and sos, Lee was a born winner and he simply would not accept defeat. His exploits for City are legendary but there was a sour end to his time at Maine Road and in 1974 when he wasn't offered the kind of package he believed he was worth, he was allowed to join Derby County. Still angry at City's decision to sell him after all he had achieved for the club, he helped inspire Derby to the league title in his first

appointment as manager was Alan Ball - a move that left many supporters underwhelmed. Unfortunately, it was a pointer to Lee's reign as chairman and he never quite delivered the goods for the fans who had helped him into power. In 1998, barely four years into his tenure, Lee was - somewhat ironically - forced to step down by fan pressure. Considering his achievements, it is, with hindsight, a pity that things turned out the way they did, though nobody can take away his loyalties and quality as a player and perhaps his spell as chairman was, if nothing else, well intentioned and with the best interests of the club at heart. Francis Lee passed away in October 2023.

RIGHT:
CHAIRMAN LEE

FAR RIGHT:
LEE LINES UP A SHOT
DURING THE FA CUP
FOURTH ROUND TIE
WITH UNITED AT
OLD TRAFFORD,
24 JAN 1970

year at the Baseball Ground and scored a blistering goal on his return to Maine Road just for good measure causing Match of the Day commentator Barry Davies to famously cry "Look at his face! Just look at his face!"

He eventually did return to City but this time as chairman. He promised much and had been the saviour of fans eager to see Peter Swales step down after many trophy-less years. The takeover battle was bitter and drawn out, but fan-power won the day and Lee was installed in his new role. The millions of pounds that were promised to buy new players never really materialised and his first

LAPORTE

Aymeric Laporte cost a club record £57m from Athletic Bilbao in January 2018. Most commonly record fees are invested in goalscorers but Laporte is a world class defender who reads the game expertly and snuffs out danger with the minimum of fuss and the maximum of effectiveness.

Strengthening an already strong squad, unsurprisingly Laporte achieved a sizeable haul of silverware in his first six with the club, with five Premier League titles, two FA Cups and three League Cups, Laporte heading the winner in the 2021 final against Spurs. He was an unused sub in the Champions League finals of 2023 and 2021.

Born in France he captained France at four junior levels up to Under 21s but then in 2021 became a full international with Spain playing at the delayed Euro 2020 tournament, scoring against Slovakia.

MAHREZ

Left-footed right-winger Riyad Mahrez was as good as any player in the Premier League when he moved from Leicester to Manchester City in July 2018 and since then he has continued to show why he is so highly rated. The fee of £60m broke both club's records as well as being the highest fee ever paid for an African player. Although born and raised in France he is an international with an Algerian father and a mother with Algerian heritage.

Riyad played for Algeria at the FIFA World Cup in 2014. They were unable to qualify for the finals four years later but in 2019 Mahrez captained his country as they defeated Senegal in the final of the African Cup of Nations.

Having attracted attention in club football in France he came to England in January 2014 as Leicester paid £450,000 to La Havre. Five years earlier he had been on a month-long trial with St Mirren where he scored seven goals in four games before infamously secretly sneaking out of Paisley to return to Paris.

While Scotland never saw the best of magnificent Mahrez England certainly has. He was a shining light in Leicester's stunning Premier League winning season in his second full season in 2015-16 when he won the PFA Players' Player of the Year award, adding the BBC African Player of the Year title at the end of the calendar year.

Since coming to Manchester Mahrez has added four further Premier League titles, three League Cups - playing in the 2021 final after being an unused sub in the previous two finals - as well as starting the 2019 FA Cup final when Watford were walloped 6-0. In 2021 Mahrez also played the full game as City played Chelsea in the Champions League final but had to be content with a place on the bench in both of the club's finals in 2023.

A fabulous footballer who is a joy to watch as he mesmerises defenders and glides beyond them, Riyad Mahrez is a flair player who helped to make Manchester City a team that at times opponents simply could not live with. Mahrez, 32, signed for Al-Ahli in July 2023 after the Saudi Arabian side agreed a €35 million deal with Manchester City.

MAINE ROAD

Home to Manchester City from 1923 until 2003, the club finally ended its 80-year tenure at the famous old ground for the last time against Southampton on 11 May 2003. City first played at their new home in 1923, just four months after Wembley Stadium was completed having left behind Hyde Road and its limited capacity. Designed by local architect Charles Swain, the original plan was for the ground to match Wembley and hold 90,000 spectators - "a stadium fit for Manchester's premier club" - as stated by officials at the time.

The opening game in August 1923 was greeted with great enthusiasm by the club's legions of fans, many of whom were in awe of its size. With only the Main Stand's 10,000 seats covered, the rest of the ground was open terracing but buoyed on by a record crowd of 56,993, the Blues beat Sheffield United 2-1 with goals from Tom Johnson and Horace Barnes. The next home game proved that the new home ground was sadly not impregnable as City lost 2-1 to Aston Villa but the club would lose just twice more at home that first season.

The 'popular side', later known as the Kippax, had a flagpole positioned roughly level with the halfway line at the very back of the terracing. Before each home game, a member of staff would proudly raise the club flag with 'City FC' emblazoned on it and then lower it after the match ended.

Surprisingly, City only once went an entire league season at Maine Road without defeat - during the 1965-66 campaign - when the club went up as Second Division champions. Maine Road saw various changes over the years but was undoubtedly most famous for its huge terrace, the Kippax, where most City fans gathered on match days. The various sands - the North Stand (formerly the Scoreboard End), Platt Lane and the Main Stand (and later, the new Kippax Stand) - were all developed at different stages over the years, giving the stadium an unusual, patched-together look.

None of the four roofs matched but that, to the supporters, was part of the charm and in many ways Maine Road's eccentric look matched the team's erratic play over the 80 years the club resided there. Shortly after the gates were locked for the final time in 2003, Maine Road was razed to the ground along with thousands of memories - happy, sad, bittersweet and joyous. Gone, but never forgotten, Maine Road will remain in City fans' hearts for many years to come.

MANCINI

One of the most recognisable people in European football, Roberto Mancini guided Italy to the European Championship in 2021, defeating England on penalties in the final. He became City boss in December 2009 and almost guided the Blues into the Champions League at the first attempt, losing out to Tottenham in a winner-takes-all clash that saw Harry Redknapp's side snatch fourth spot.

Mancini set about rebuilding his team, adding Yaya Toure, Mario Balotelli, Edin Dzeko and David Silva to his side and then watched his team life their first trophy since 1976 with a 1-0 win over Stoke City in the 2011 FA Cup Final. City also finished in third position in the Premier League and qualified for Champions League football for the first time - the Blues' boss was on track to become the most successful manger since Joe Mercer in the late 1960s.

But there was even better to come. With Sergio Aguero, Samir Nasri and Gael Clichy all added to the squad during the summer of 2011, City raced out of the blocks and challenged for the top spot in the table with Manchester United from the very first game. The pivotal moment of the campaign came when City destroyed United 6-1 at Old Trafford - sending out a message to their neighbours that the Blues were no longer prepared to stand in the shadow of their oldest foes.

The battle continued until, with six games to go, City fell eight points behind United to the title race. It seemed all over and Mancini publicly conceded the title to United - but privately he still believed it was possible. Somehow, City closed the deficit and went into the final game against QPR knowing a victory would win the Premier League title - in the most dramatic of circumstances, the Blues did exactly that when Aguero scored in the dying minutes to ensure Mancini's place in the club's folklore.

Sacked two days after losing the 2013 FA Cup final with Wigan, Mancini signed off in the sort of style he is synonymous with by taking out a full page ad in the Manchester Evening News to thank the club's fans for their support. Ciao Roberto!

MARSH

Controversy, terrific individual skill and frustration - the mercurial Rodney Marsh had the City fans eating out of his hand and tearing out their hair in equal measures for much of his time at the club. Signed from QPR to boost City's 1972 title run-in, he was blamed by many for City's disappointing finish to the season. Despite playing during a period packed with personalities and stars, his sublime skills and invention still shone brightly and he went on to play 142 times for the Blues, scoring on 46 occasions.

A fall-out with boss Tony Book led to him being dropped from the first team and he was transfer-listed after being accused of not giving 100 per cent - something he vehemently denied. He almost moved to Anderlecht during November 1975 after the two clubs agreed a fee but he decided the language could be a problem and stayed at Maine Road, training with the youth team until the dispute was settled. In 1976 he finally ended his City career by moving to Tampa Bay Rowdies as one of the first English players to join the blossoming NASL.

He continued to sparkle throughout his career and during a brief period of time with Fulham in the mid-Seventies (along with George Best) he produced showmanship of the highest calibre. After retiring as a player Marsh continued to support QPR and Manchester City. Today he is now a co-host for a radio show called 'Grumpy Pundits'.

McDOWALL

Les McDowall spent a fair proportion of his life employed by Manchester City - 24 years in fact - though his playing days were truncated by the second world war. Born in Gunga Pur, India, it was the 1930s' Depression that first brought McDowall into the spotlight. An aircraft draughtsman, he was laid off due to lack of wood and was playing a match with other unemployed men, when a scout from Sunderland spotted him. He signed for Sunderland and played 13 games for the Roker Park team until City came in with a bid of around £7,500 in 1938.

Within a year McDowall was made skipper of the Blues up until war broke out, ironically putting his football career on hold while he returned to his former trade. Times changed and following the war he handed over the captaincy to Sam Barkas and not long after he was briefly appointed manager of Wrexham. A little over a year later, City returned for their former captain - this time with the offer of being manager with the immediate challenge of hauling the club out of Division Two. It would be a historic appointment in many ways as his tenure was never short of excitement and drama.

In charge for some 13 years, he was also, behind Wilf Wild, just one year short of managing the club for a record length of time.

Never afraid to adopt innovative ideas, he was in charge when the famous 'Revie Plan' was instigated and he began his reign with instant promotion. He also tried the little publicised 'Marsden Plan' which involved Keith Marsden acting as a sweeper. City lost 6-1 to Preston and 9-2 to West Brom and the plan was indefinitely shelved! More positively, the club went on the successive FA Cup Finals in 1955 and 1956 under McDowall; the latter of which was victorious. Players such as Denis Law were signed during his reign and in 1960 Law's £55,000 transfer fee was a British record. City were eventually relegated under McDowall and in 1963, after presiding over an incredible 546 league games, he left for Oldham Athletic, where he stayed for two years. He died in 1991, aged 78.

MERCER

Regarded by many as one of the greatest wing-halves of his day, Joe Mercer was an Everton player from 1932 to 1947, collecting a League championship medal in 1939. The war stole many years from his career and when the League resumed, things had changed at Goodison Park and he moved to Highbury.

With Arsenal he went on to even greater glory, including two more league championships plus another winners' medal for clinching the FA Cup. A broken leg forced retirement and robbed him of yet more playing years. His first move into management was with Sheffield United and he impressed sufficiently to be later installed as Aston Villa boss. He took them to promotion from Division Two, won the League Cup and led them to two FA Cup semi-finals. The pressures and stress of management took their toll on him and he suffered a minor stroke, threatening his future in the game he had already given up so much to. Fortunately, fate had cleared a path that would take him on to greater heights, and after the doctors gave him a clean bill of health, the Villa board duly sacked him.

He decided to retire and many thought they had seen the last of 'Genial Joe'. But Mercer's love of the game pulled him back and in 1965, when Manchester City offered him the chance of waking a sleeping giant, he grabbed it with both hands.

His first decision as Blues' boss was also arguably his best, bringing in upcoming coach Malcolm Allison as his assistant and though the pair were alike as chalk and cheese, they would prove the perfect managerial team. Within a year, Mercer's new-look City had won the Division Two title, and two years later the Blues were crowned champions of England for only the second time in the club's history, winning the First Division with the style and panache the supporters demanded.

The trophies just kept on coming. The FA Cup in 1969, the League Cup in 1970 and later that same season, the first and only European trophy City have won - the Cup Winners' Cup - was brought back to Manchester by Mercer and his talented troops. Five trophies in five years - an incredible return. Malcolm Allison was involved in some bitter arguments with the City board and in 1970 he was very nearly sacked, but, with Mercer's backing, Allison remained at the club. City almost added another league title in season 1971-72 but Allison's idea of bringing in Rodney Marsh backfired and City lost pole position to end fourth in one of the tightest top-flight finishes ever. After seven years as number two, Allison seemingly manipulated events that led top Mercer leaving his position and eventually joining Coventry City in 1972. Allison believed he deserved a chance to call the shots himself and though no-one would have denounced his ambition, many fans were upset by the events leading to Mercer's departure.

A general manager at Coventry, he became England boss on a temporary basis in 1974 in order to, as he put it himself, "try and restore some laughter' following the national side's omission from the World Cup qualifiers. He was deservedly awarded the OBE in 1976 for services to football and he remained a director at Highfield Road until his resignation in 1981. He retired to his beloved Merseyside and died in August 1990. A legendary and much-loved figure to all Manchester City fans, the club named an access road to the ground as 'Joe Mercer Way'.

MANAGER JOE MERCER SHOWS OFF THE FA CUP FOLLOWING THE 1-0 WIN OVER LEICESTER CITY SURROUNDED BY HIS TRIUMPHANT TEAM

MEREDITH

Born in Chirk, North Wales, Billy Meredith used to cycle from his tiny mining village to Hyde Road to play for City and then cycled home afterwards. He was also without doubt, one of the greatest players ever to represent Manchester City. Meredith was something of a controversial character but is ranked by many alongside the great Sir Stanley Matthews in stature and an icon for all football fans and the media in his day. Bandy-legged and invariably chewing a toothpick, he was the scourge of many an Edwardian defender.

The immensely-talented right winger could pinpoint a cross for the forwards or cut inside and lash the ball home himself if the mood took him and despite hugging the touchline for much of the game, with 151 goals for the club, he is among City's all-time top scorers. He was involved in a bribe and illegal payment scandal that rocked the club to its foundations and subsequently joined Manchester United helping them to great success before finally returning to City in 1921.

He also won 22 Welsh caps as a City Player and holds the record for being the oldest footballer to turn out for the Blues. He was aged just 120 days short of his 50th birthday when he played his last game for the club - a 2-0 defeat to Newcastle United in an FA Cup semi-final. Meredith was also a founder member of the PFA (Professional Football Association) more than 100 years ago.

NAVAS

Born in Los Palacios on 21 November 1985 Spain international Jesus Navas spent four years with City in between two successful spells with Seville. Including two FIFA World Cup qualifying games for his country Navas made 50 appearances in his first season, helping City to the Premier League title and League (Capital One) Cup, scoring the killer third goal in a 3-1 Wembley win over Sunderland when his pace told in a last-minute break. Two years later he won the League Cup gain, scoring in a penalty shoot-out as Liverpool were defeated.

In total Navas started 117 games for City and came off the bench a further 66 times while scoring eight goals. Before coming to Manchester, he had played 323 times for Seville, all but 30 of those being starts. To the summer of 2023, he had made 508+63 appearances for the Spanish club. Twice a Europa League winner in his first spell with Seville he won it again in 2020 and 2023 to add to his two Copa del Rey titles there as well as the Spanish and UEFA Supercups.

NASRI

Samir Nasri started 99 Premier League games for Manchester City. He played a further 30 times as a substitute in the Premier League and in total made 135+41 appearances scoring 27 times. A classy player with an eye for a telling pass he established his creativity with a hat-trick of assists on his debut as Spurs were taken apart 5-1 in August 2011. Man of the Match in the 2014 League (Capital One) Cup final when he scored a 'worldie' against Sunderland he also won Premier League titles with City in 2012 and 2014.

Born on 26 June 1987 in Septemes-les-Vallons, Nasri won 41 caps for France, scoring one of his five goals against England at Euro 2012. He also played for Marseille, Arsenal, Antalyaspor, West Ham and Anderlecht as well as having a loan from City to Seville but in 2018 blotted his copybook by receiving a UEFA ban for a doping offence in 2016. Nasri protested his innocence insisting he didn't know the rules but nonetheless served an 18-month suspension.

OAKES

Alan Oakes gave solid, reliable service to Manchester City for more than 18 years. With 669 first-team appearances, he is the record appearance holder and unlikely ever to be surpassed. Surprisingly overlooked at International level for England, due almost entirely to the fact that he played a similar role to Bobby Moore, Oakes was every bit as important to City as Moore was to West Ham.

His cousin was another unsung hero from the same era, Glyn Pardoe. Best known for his surging runs from deep and penetrative passes, Oakes was happy to let others take the limelight yet was vital to the all-conquering Mercer side of the late 1960s and the management showed their faith in Oakes by naming him captain for the 1968-69 season in Tony Book's absence. He almost won international recognition when he was one of several City players named in the original squad of 40 for the 1970 World Cup but missed out on a trip to Mexico when the final squad was named. Consistent up until the end of his days at Maine Road, he was named Player of the Year in 1975 just a year before he left City for Chester, where he eventually became player-manager of the club and added another 211 appearances to his evergreen career.

OASIS FANS FILL THE GROUND
AT MAINE ROAD, APRIL 1996

OASIS

Burnage-born brothers Noel and Liam Gallagher, the driving force behind the legendary rock band Oasis, are arguably City's most famous and vocal supporters. During the mid-1990s the band and the club enjoyed a healthy association, lending branding and such like to one another in a mutually beneficial relationship.

For a while, City ran out to 'Roll With It' and it was rare for an Oasis track not to be played during the half-time break at Maine Road. The Gallaghers walked out on the pitch on several occasions and Noel even had a specially made 'MCFC' guitar. In 1995, the City supporters turned their classic "Wonderwall" into a swooning tribute to Georgi

Kinkladze and Alan Ball, though Noel commented that he wasn't too happy about the Alan Ball verse! The mutual admiration between band and club reached epidemic proportions when Oasis played several sold-out gigs at Maine Road in 1996 and were once even touted as potential owners.

Though the band has disbanded and the brothers now live in London, they still regularly attend both home and away matches and their love affair with the club still burns brightly. In 2021, the romance was reciprocated as City became champions and a video emerged of Pep Guardiola and his staff celebrating as they sang 'Don't look Back In Anger'.

PARDOE

Though Glyn Pardoe played in almost every position for City during his long career, it was left-back that was his preferred role. The cousin of another City great, Alan Oakes, Pardoe was also part of the all-conquering City side of the late 1960s and early '70s that swept all before them. Like Oakes, Pardoe was born in Winsford and joined City from Mid-Cheshire Boys. Arguably his finest moment came when he scored the winner in the **1970 League Cup Final, one of only 22 City goals.**

He was desperately unlucky when he broke his leg in the Manchester derby later that same year, following a challenge from George Best, and never managed to fully reclaim his left-back berth owing to the form of youngster Willie Donachie. The holder of two unique records, being the youngest player ever to play for the Blues aged just 15 and 341 days when he debuted against Birmingham City on 11 April 1962; and he was also the Blues first ever substitute (unused) for the opening game of 1965-66. He later became a hugely successful youth-team coach at Maine Road following his retirement in 1976, helping guide the young Blues to win the 1986 FA Youth Cup. An underrated footballer, Pardoe passed away in May 2020, aged 73.

PAUL

Manchester City's very own Captain Fantastic, Roy Paul was an inspirational figure to colleagues and fans alike, captaining the Blues to the 1955 FA Cup Final, where they lost to Newcastle United. The hard as nails leader vowed to return to win the cup the following year and, true to his word, the former coal miner drove the Blues on to the 1956 FA Cup final after threatening to clip around the ear anyone who did not pull their weight.

It worked, and this time City were victorious over Birmingham City. Paul, who handed out his own brand of justice on the pitch - albeit always fairly - had arrived from Swansea Town in 1950 and was versatile in that he could play anywhere along the back line. A true 'Roy of the Rovers' type of player, Paul was one of the greatest captains the club ever had and he was the second Welshman to skipper the Blues to FA Cup glory - the first being Billy Meredith. Paul left for Worcester City in June 1957 after clocking up nearly 300 appearances for City. He died in the spring of 2002.

PENALTIES

City have had their moments from the penalty spot, both good and bad. In 1912, City managed to miss three penalties in one game! Irvine Thornley and Eli Fletcher (twice) were the guilty parties and the game with Newcastle United ended 1-1. It was again Newcastle who were the opposition on an unfortunate day from the spot, this time for Billy Austin, when in 1926, the Blues, who needed a point to avoid relegation, after five successive wins, missed from the spot and lost 3-2 and were subsequently relegated!

Ken Barnes scored a hat-trick of penalties against Everton in December 1957 in a 6-2 win and scored another in the return fixture at Goodison Park. Mention penalties to any City fan, however, and chances are talk will quickly turn to Franny Lee - the club's most successful penalty taker ever with 46 successive spot-kicks put away in his time at Maine Road. Lee won many of his penalties and was deadly from the spot, including several double strikes.

Kevin Bond once scored penalties in the 44th and 45th minutes of a home game against Huddersfield Town, In 2006, Arsenal were awarded a penalty against City and

Thierry Henry ran up, tapped the ball forward for Robert Pires to put past David James - at least that was what was meant to happen. They made a hash of the chance and Danny Mills cleared the ball downfield. Though the City players were furious at such a disrespectful act, the Blues had actually done something similar more than 40 years before. In March 1960 when Denis Law made his home debut against West Ham and with City trailing 1-0, Law was fouled in the box and the Blues were awarded a penalty.

Ken Barnes placed the ball on the spot, ran up and tapped it forward for Billy McAdams to run from behind and tuck the ball away. The referee gave the goal but amid furious protests from the Hammers, he consulted a linesman and ordered the kick to be retaken. Barnes stepped up again and missed. Fortunately, City went on to win 3-1.

City can also boast the most successful penalty taker ever in their hall of fame. Yaya Toure, who played more than 300 games for the club between 2010 and 2018 is a notable candidate for the "Penalty King" tag. In his career, Yaya took 16 penalties in official competitive games, and did not miss a single one. Quite astonishing.

SUCCESS FROM THE SPOT AGAINST SPURS AT WHITE HART LANE, JANUARY 2014

TOMMY CATON

PLAYER OF THE YEAR

The following is a list of the Player of the Year Awards that began at the competition of the **1966-67** season, as voted for by the club's supporters.

1966-67	TONY BOOK		1981-82	TOMMY CATON
1967-68	COLIN BELL		1982-83	KEVIN BOND
1968-69	GLYN PARDOE		1983-84	MICK McCARTHY
1969-70	FRANCIS LEE		1984-85	PAUL POWER
1970-71	MIKE DOYLE		1985-86	KENNY CLEMENTS
1971-72	MIKE SUMMERBEE		1986-87	NEIL MCNAB
1972-73	MIKE SUMMERBEE		1987-88	STEVE REDMOND
1973-74	MIKE DOYLE		1988-89	NEIL McNAB
1974-75	ALAN OAKES		1989-90	COLIN HENDRY
1975-76	JOE CORRIGAN		1990-91	NIALL QUINN
1976-77	DAVE WATSON		1991-92	TONY COTON
1977-78	JOE CORRIGAN		1992-93	GARRY FLITCROFT
1978-79	ASA HARTFORD		1993-94	TONY COTON
1979-80	JOE CORRIGAN		1994-95	UWE ROSLER
1980-81	PAUL POWER		1995-96	GIO KINKLADZE

1996-97	GIO KINKLADZE
1997-98	MICHAEL BROWN
1998-99	GERARD WIEKENS
1990-2000	SHAUN GOATER
2000-01	DANNY TIATO
2001-02	ALI BENARBIA
2002-03	SYLVAIN DISTIN
2003-04	SHAUN WRIGHT-PHILIPS
2004-05	RICHARD DUNNE
2005-06	RICHARD DUNNE
2006-07	RICHARD DUNNE
2007-08	RICHARD DUNNE
2008-09	STEPHEN IRELAND
2009-10	CARLOS TEVEZ
2010-11	VINCENT KOMPANY
2011-12	SERGIO AGUERO
2012-13	PABLO ZABALETA
2013-14	YAYA TOURE
2014-15	SERGIO AGUERO

2015-16	KEVIN DE BRUYNE
2016-17	DAVID SILVA
2017-18	KEVIN DE BRUYNE
2018-19	BERNARDO SILVA
2019-20	KEVIN DE BRUYNE
2020-21	RUBEN DIAS
2021-22	KEVIN DE BRUYNE
2022-23	ERLING HAALAND

KEVIN DE BRUYNE

LEFT:
SERGIO AGUERO

POWER

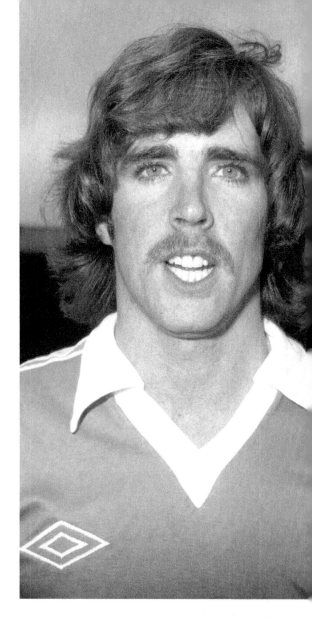

Paul Power was arguably one of the hardest working City players ever to pull on a blue shirt. He captained the club for many years earning respect throughout the game for being one of the most dedicated professionals in football. The left-sided midfielder might not have been a prolific scorer for the Blues but he is best remembered by City fans for two incredible goals he scored during his time with the club.

His wonderful solo goal against AC Milan in 1978 in the San Siro Stadium gave the Blues a vital edge in a difficult UEFA Cup tie and his superb curling free-kick against Ipswich in the 1981 FA Cup semi-final sent City to face Tottenham in the Centenary Cup Final. His services were rewarded by City supporters who twice voted him Player of the Year - and he captained the Blues in three Wembley finals - twice against Spurs in the FA Cup and once against Chelsea in the Full Members' Cup. An intelligent and thoughtful man, he qualified in law after completing his studies in 1975.

He was sold to Everton by manager Billy McNeil in June 1986 and waited only 12 months before he picked up his first League Championship medal with the Toffees. Always with City at heart Paul spent many years working behind the scenes coaching at the City academy before spending his retirement living in France.

PREMIER LEAGUE

Champions in 2023 for the ninth time, this is the golden age of City who up to 2011 had been champions of England just twice. Eric Brook was the leading light when the Championship came to the club for the first time in 1936-37. The glorious era of the late sixties peaked in 1967-68 when a last day 4-3 win at Newcastle once again secured the title.

Well over four decades passed until another league title came to Manchester City in the shape of a first Premier League success. It couldn't have come in more dramatic fashion as in the dying seconds of the season not one but two injury time goals turned defeat to victory against QPR and with it the joy of proclaiming Manchester City as Premier League champions.

Since that day the Premier League trophy has made the Etihad Stadium its second home. Champions again two years later in 2014, in 2018 a magnificent 100 points brought the title back to the club who retained it the following year with another incredible points tally of 98. After relinquishing their grip on the trophy in 2020 when Pep Guardiola's side were runners-up a third title in four years was secured in 2021 with a third successive Premier League title secured in 2023. Having now joined Everton as champions of England on nine occasions there are only three clubs to have been champions more often than City.

CITY LIFT THE 2022-23 PREMIER LEAGUE TROPHY AS THEY ARE CROWNED CHAMPIONS FOR THE THIRD CONSECUTIVE SEASON

QUINN

Niall Quinn joined from Arsenal for a bargain £800,000 in 1989 and went on to become one of the most popular players ever to wear the No 9 shirt for the club. His skilful and intelligent link-up play belied his inelegant 6ft 4in frame, with his deft flicks, chips and cushioned headers backed by excellent technique.

He was often a valuable extra defender at set pieces and corners, and one abiding memory City fans have of 'Quinny' was the time he took over in goal during a home match with Derby County after keeper Tony Coton had brought down Dean Saunders and was shown a red card. With no goalie on the bench, Quinn, a former Gaelic football player, put on the green jersey to face a penalty kick. With the whole of Maine Road willing him on, he guessed right and saved the penalty from Saunders! His two goals in the final match of the same season relegated Sunderland, the club he would eventually join in 1996 and become chairman of a decade later.

Quinn also commendably donated the entire proceeds of his testimonial - believed to have been around £1million - to charity. An excellent servant for Manchester City, Ireland and the game of football.

QUOTES

KEVIN KEEGAN

People always have plenty to say about Manchester City. Here are some notable comments on the club:

"I always kind of knew that 40 years of loyalty would be repaid somehow and I always knew that a day would come when we stagger everyone in football. It'll be nice to know that every gallon of petrol a Manchester United fans buys is going into our transfer kitty."

NOEL GALLAGHER

"[City's] ambitions are large and unlimited."

SHEIKH MANSOUR (November 2013)

"We went out believing we could beat anybody. It didn't matter who we turned out against. The team talks were very limited, 'Get out there and play. You're better than they are."

COLIN BELL on Joe Mercer

"Sometimes you have to shoot at the stars and maybe you'll hit the moon."

KEVIN KEEGAN

"He can't head it. He can't pass it and he's no good on his left foot"

MALCOLM ALLISON on Colin Bell before he signed him, trying to put other suitors off.

"I have to hold my hands up. I cost Manchester City the 1972 league championship."

RODNEY MARSH

"There is a real soul about this club."

VINCENT KOMPANY

REID

When Howard Kendall became City manager in November 1989, he had only one man in mind to lead his side out of the relegation battle - Peter Reid. Installed as a player/coach, Reid had the natural leadership qualities that City desperately needed, and though he may have had his best years elsewhere, the gutsy little midfielder, never gave less than his all for City and the fans loved him for it.

Reid held together a young midfield and influenced a side having something of a reputation of a soft centre, into a tight, difficult-to-beat dogs of war outfit and when Kendall quit the Blues just after a year in charge, Reid seemed the natural successor and by popular demand, he became the club's first player/manager, guiding them to successive fifth-placed finishes in the league.

Things turned sour for Reid when, it is alleged, the board asked him to dispense with the services of his coach Sam Ellis, the man the City fans blamed for the long ball-game City were playing at the time. Reid refused to be forced into a corner and was sacked as a result, loyally standing by Ellis.

Reid later re-surfaced at Sunderland for whom he bought Niall Quinn from City. He led the club as they moved from Roker Park to the Stadium of Light, welcoming City for the first game at the latter and winning the Championship at both stadia, achieving 105 points in 1998-99.

REVIE

Later famed as manager of Leeds United and England, Don Revie played more games for Manchester City than any of his other four clubs. Debuting at Burnley on 20 October 1951 he went on to play 172 games in all competitions, scoring 41 times. However, facts and figures do not begin to reveal Revie's influence on the side. Renowned for his tactical awareness as a manager Revie's footballing brain had been seen as a player.

It was the 'Revie Plan' named after him that transformed City in the mid-fifties. It saw Don operate as a deep-lying centre-forward pulling the opposition's centre-half out of position. Manager Les McDowall masterminded the system and stuck with it when its first use ended in a 5-0 defeat at Preston North End. Second time out there were signs of success as Revie scored twice in a 5-2 win over Sheffield United. City went on to reach the FA Cup final two years running, winning the second of those finals with Revie having been named Footballer of the Year in the first year of the plan named in his honour.

A goal on Don's debut for England against Northern Ireland in October 1954 was the first of four goals in six games for his country. He later went on to manage England only to leave in sensationally controversial circumstances to take up a lucrative job managing the United Arab Emirates. It was a move that saw the FA hand him a decade-long ban for bringing the game into disrepute.

REVIE ON THE TRAINING GROUND, MAY 1955

RICHARDS

Now a regular TV pundit and enthusiastic follower of City, Micah made his name after bursting onto the scene as a 17-year-old. An outstanding Academy player, he made his Premiership debut against Arsenal in October 2005, aged 17.

He first came to the attention of the nation when he scored a last-minute equaliser for City in an FA Cup tie at Aston Villa and promptly swore during the after-match interview! A powerfully-built lad, he was comfortable in virtually any position and his whirlwind rise to the top continued when he was awarded a full cap against Holland during the 2006-07 season, becoming the youngest defender ever to play for England.

Richards was an integral part of City's defence during his first full season, winning plaudits throughout the game for his strength and athleticism. He was also the youngest nominee for the PFA's Young Player of the Year Award in 2007 and 2008.

All 13 of his England caps were won with City who he left to join Aston Villa after a loan spell with Fiorentina. He made 164+15 appearances for City during which he scored seven goals and also represented Great Britain at the 2012 Olympics. His friendly on-screen relationship with fellow pundit Roy Keane has made them an unlikely partnership that has endeared them to the nation's football fans, especially those of City and United.

RODRI

The hero of Istanbul with the goal that won the Champions League for City, Rodri was totally immense in City's treble-winning campaign of 2022-23. Playing the often dictatorial role of holding midfielder, during the season Rodri made 4,068 passes, that's 888 more than Ruben Dias who made the next highest number. While Erling Haaland and Kevin De Bruyne often took the headlines by topping the goal and assist charts Rodri was not just the pass master - he also made the most tackles (108) and duels (277). A real team player who got his big moment in the limelight with that winning goal against Inter.

Born in Madrid on 22 June 1996, Roderigo Hernández Cascante played youth football for Rayo Majadahonda, Atlético Madrid and Villareal, making his senior debut for the latter in December 2015 against SD Huesca. After 61+23 games and a couple of goals he moved to Atlético Madrid in the summer of 2018 but after just one season where he scored three times in 41+6 appearances he found himself destined for Manchester and ultimately a place in City folklore.

ROSLER

German striker Uwe Rosler - 'Der Bomber' - was ironically, a typically English centre-forward whose bustling energetic style made his £500,000 fee from FC Nurnberg look like peanuts after finishing top scorer in three of four seasons with the Blues. The fans immediately identified with Rosler's passion and he became a huge crowd idol on the Kippax with his strike partnership with Paul Walsh particularly profitable, especially when served by a constant stream of superb crosses from wingers Peter Beagrie and Nicky Summerbee.

Rosler was lethal in the air and went on to win caps for Germany after winning several from East Germany prior to unification. He returned home to play for Kaiserslautern after City were relegated to Division Two in 1998 but failed to repeat the heroics he showed while at Maine Road with either them, West Brom or Southampton. Rosler made a successful recovery from chest cancer while playing for Lillestrom in Norway and would later manage the same club. He has gone on to manage Brentford, Wigan, Leeds and Fleetwood as well as Malmo in Sweden and Fortuna Dusseldorf in Germany.

ROYLE

Signed from Everton on Christmas Eve 1974 for £200,000, Joe Royle became an integral part of Tony Book's successful mid-1970s side, leading the line bravely and often being the foil for Dennis Tueart or Brian Kidd. Never a prolific scorer with just one goal from 16 games - it was to be his one failing during his time with the Blues as a player, where he averaged just one every four games.

After leaving City he played for Bristol City and Norwich before moving into management with Oldham Athletic, where he transformed a music hall joke into one of the most respected sides in the country. He later managed Everton, guiding them to an FA Cup final before taking charge of City in 1998. Though he seemed to arrive with time to save the club, City were still relegated and Royle and his assistant Willie Donachie began to trim the unusually large squad and build a new one from scratch. He sold fan's favourite Gio Kinkladze to Ajax for £5.5 million while the likes of Andy Morrison, Ian Bishop and Shaun Goater were all recruited for less than half a million pounds in total.

Under Royle, City would then secure back-to-back promotions after beating Gillingham in the Division Two Play-Off final and finishing runners-up to Charlton Athletic the following season. Royle was a hero and could do little wrong in the supporters' eyes. With the likes of George Weah and Paulo Wanchope signed during the summer of 2000, the Blues faced life in the Premiership with confidence, but ten months later City had been relegated. Although City went down, it still came as a surprise when Royle was sacked in May 2001. He went on to manage Ipswich and have a second spell in charge of Oldham before becoming a director of Wigan Athletic.

SILVA

City signed Bernardo Silva in July 2017 after he helped Monaco to the Ligue 1 title and a hugely impressive run to the Champions League semi-finals. Blessed with balance, guile and great technique the Portuguese midfielder was nicknamed 'Bubblegum' due to the way the ball sticks to his feet on mazy dribbles.

In an impressive first season, he netted nine times and had 11 assists as he ended the campaign with a Premier League and Carabao Cup medal. His second season in Manchester proved even better on both a personal and team level. City swept all before them domestically and the then 24-year-old was sensational throughout. He recorded 13 goals and 14 assists in 51 appearances, winning Man of the Match in the Carabao Cup final win over Chelsea and ending the campaign as the Club's Player of the Season.

In 2019-20, he made 52 appearances and scored eight goals - his third campaign in a row that he clocked up a half century or more games for the Club. He was again integral to the City team in the 2020-21 season, making 45 appearances to take his club total to 201 - an average of 50.25 games per campaign.

The 2021-22 season proved to be another magnificent one for the popular midfielder. As well as winning three successive Etihad Player of the Season votes, he played 50 times and equalled his best goals tally with 13. He had the distinction, in March's 2-0 home win over Newcastle United, of scoring City's 1,000th home goal in the Premier League era.

The Portugal international continued to be a key figure in the 2022-23 campaign to help the club lift their third consecutive Premier League title while he also played in the 2-1 win over Manchester United in the FA Cup final to help City win it for the second time under Pep. Silva played another crucial game in the 1-0 win over Inter in the Champions League final to help City secure the Treble in his seventh season with the club.

SILVA

The unveiling of a statue to Silva in August 2021 illustrated how valued 'El Mago' is at City where his magical ability on the ball made him a key man in a decade of unprecedented success where Silva cemented his place as a City icon.

David Josue Jimenez Silva made a total of 436 appearances for the club, scoring 77 goals and being credited with 92 Premier League assists. Born in Gran Canaria on 8 January 1986 David arrived in Manchester in the summer of 2010 shortly after being part of the Spain squad that won the FIFA World Cup. At international level he won 125 caps and scored 35 times.

Players' Player of the Year at City in 2012 and Player of the Year five years later Silva was also twice selected for the Premier League Team of the Year. He won four Premier League titles, two FA Cups and five League Cups with the club having already won the Copa Del Rey with Valencia before coming to England. He returned to Spain in 2020 with Real Sociedad.

STERLING

Born in Kingston Jamaica on 8 December 1994, Raheem became one of the most lethal and exciting forwards in the game. Always noted for his exceptional pace, Sterling's finishing has improved over the years, especially since his record £44m transfer deal prised him from Liverpool in July 2015 after he had been the Anfielders' Player of the Season for the past two years.

A major influence in City's success Sterling had won four Premier League crowns, five League Cups and the FA Cup by 2022. Appointed an MBE for his services to racial equality in sport in 2021, two years earlier he had been the Football Writers' Association Footballer of the Year and a nominee for the Ballon d'Or. That same season he also scored twice in the FA Cup final a 6-0 hammering of Watford in 2019. Initially he had been thought to have become only the fourth player to score a hat-trick at the show-piece occasion only for a goal many thought Raheem had scored to be credited to Gabriel Jesus.

In the summer of 2022 Sterling switched to Chelsea for a reported £47.5m, making 23 Premier League starts in his first season at Stamford Bridge.

For England, Raheem debuted as a 17-year-old away to Sweden in November 2014. To July 2023 he had won 82 caps and scored 20 goals for his country.

STONES

A product of Barnsley's academy, John Stones built a reputation of an assured ball-playing centre-half with Everton before signing for City in August 2016. Already an England international, he has since won every domestic honour available with the Blues.

A solid first season saw Stones make 41 appearances while he turned out 29 times to help City lift the 2017-18 Premier League and Carabao Cup - his first taste of success at senior level - and win a place in England's 2018 World Cup squad.

Injury again affected him the following season, though he remained an important figure within the team, featuring in 39 games. He missed the Carabao Cup final but played in the Community Shield and FA Cup wins and made a vital goal line clearance to help City beat Liverpool in January 2018's title showdown at the Etihad Stadium.

Injuries restricted him to just 24 games in 2019-20 but the 2020-21 season proved to be a memorable one. His form and partnership with new signing Ruben Dias formed the backbone of City superb mid-season run of victories that took the Blues to the summit of the Premier League.

Having rediscovered his best form, he played 35 times for City and scored five goals as well as winning his England place back for Euro 2020. He re-established himself as one of the best defenders in Europe and only injury set-backs prevented him from playing more than he did in 2021-22.

He evolved into a world class player 2022-23 campaign, performing with great distinction at right back and the centre of defence while also going forward more regularly into the midfield where his ability to run with the ball and passing has been breath-taking at times.

He notably scored in a 4-1 win over Arsenal, one of ten consecutive wins for City, which helped the club snatch its third consecutive Premier League title. The England stalwart had a stand-out performance in City's 2-1 win over Manchester United in the FA Cup final while he played for the majority of the 1-0 win over Inter in the Champions League final to help City win their first-ever Treble.

SUMMERBEE

Mike Summerbee is one of the (if not the) greatest wingers that has played for Manchester City. 'Buzzer' - - as one and all knew him - was a vital member of the Joe Mercer side of the late 1960s and his contribution to the Blues' halcyon days was immense. Adored by the crowd, especially the Kippax, Summerbee played the game with good humour and was happy to entertain the Maine Road faithful with or without the ball, though his professionalism and will to win were never compromised in the least.

With Colin Bell and Franny Lee, he was part of the so called "Holy Trinity" that inspired City to sustained success. Along with Lee, he became one of the first attackers to defend from the front, often seeking out his marker early on and then launching into a crunching tackle. With Summerbee there was never a dull moment.

Though far from a prolific scorer, he made many goals for others and he was also the first City star to be voted Player of the Year for two years running in 1972 and 1973.

Something of a dedicated follower of fashion, he owned a successful shirt-tailoring company for many years and also co-owned a fashion boutique with his friend George Best, but it will always be on the pitch that the former England star will be best remembered.

Capped eight times by England he also played for Swindon Town, Burnley, Blackpool and Stockport County where he became player/manager. His son Nicky, father George and uncle Gordon were also footballers. As of 2021 Mike is a very popular Manchester City Club Ambassador.

SWIFT

Signed from non-league Fleetwood Town after he had written to Manchester City to ask for a trial, Frank Swift's career spanned 17 years at the club. Swift was only the second goalkeeper to captain England and was the innovator of many unorthodox ideas including the long throw-out instead of a hoof up the pitch - Swift could comfortably grip the ball in one hand.

He enjoyed a run of four seasons when he was an ever-present in the team and would have been likely to have held the record number of appearances for City but for the unavoidable break of seven seasons due to the second world war. Swift was a gentle giant and was adored by the supporters, especially the youngsters who idolised him.

He retired in 1949 and was replaced by Bert Trautmann, eventually moving into journalism. It was after covering Manchester United's game in Yuogoslavia that one of City's greatest ever players lost his life in the 1958 Munich air disaster - a tragic end to a hugely talented and popular man.

TEVEZ

One thing you could confidently say about Carlos Tevez's time with City - there was never a dull moment. The Argentine striker arrived in 2009 in a deal that stunned football with the player unable to agree a deal with Manchester United - his loan club for two years.

Famously, a poster appeared around Manchester with 'Welcome to Manchester' emblazoned on it - as City entered a new era under Abu Dhabi-based owners.

Tevez proved an instant hit in his first season, scoring 29 goals in 42 games and after taking on the captaincy, hit another 23 goals in 42 starts the next season. However, his third season was blighted by controversy.

Having had a transfer request turned down, he refused to warm-up during a Champions League game with Bayern Munich and he was told he would never again play for the club. Following a three-month hiatus in Argentina, bridges were rebuilt and the player returned at the back end of the 2011-12 campaign, scoring a hat-trick away to Norwich and playing his part in the eventual title win.

He continued in the 2012-13 season with goals in his first four games as he scored 17 times to take his City tally to 74 goals in 125+23 games. South American Footballer of the Year three times, Carlos Tevez was a live-wire wherever he went.

TOSELAND

Ernie Toseland joined City from Coventry in 1929 after scoring 11 goals in 22 appearances for the Sky Blues. The flying winger then went on to become a vital part of the Blues' championship and FA Cup-winning side of the 1930s. Unlucky to never win full England honours, Toseland was at his peak at a time of many other great wingers and he never had the chance to shine on an international stage.

He rarely missed a game during his time at Maine Road and his goal tally regularly reached double figures for the Blues. He played in successive FA Cup finals for City in 1933 and 1934, scoring four times and playing in all rounds during the successful return to Wembley against Portsmouth. Along with Eric Brook, Alec Herd and Red Tilson, Toseland forged one of the most feared attacks in the game and with more than 400 appearances for City over a ten-year period, he was also one of the club's greats servants.

TOURE

It's probably fair to say that Yaya Toure was considered a decent player during his time at Barcelona. Not a regular but more than capable whenever called upon.

For his true worth and value, it took a move to City to show the world he was actually one of the best midfielders of his generation. It took about a third of the season for YaYa to move into top gear but when he did, he took some stopping. Few players in the world had the same ability to drive a team forward with such power and brute strength as Yaya.

A wonderful passer, he went on to win three Premier League titles, the FA Cup and two League Cups, his wonder-goal in the 2014 Capital One Cup final against Sunderland turning the tie.

In total, Yaya turned out 316 times for City including 24 appearances as sub. He scored 81 goals but more than that it was his power, presence and poise that helped City to dominate so many matches where he was the key man.

TRAUTMANN

Bert Trautmann overcame a whole host of incredible obstacles to become one of the most popular players to play for the Blues. A German paratrooper during the second world war, Trautmann was captured in Normandy and then made a prisoner of war. While at the POW camp in Ashton-in-Makerfield, he tried his hand at goalkeeping. His training as a paratrooper had served him well, as he would later claim that it helped him dive around fearlessly without getting hurt.

When he was released after the war, he decided to stay in England, eventually finding work on a farm. He played for St Helens FC and shortly afterwards married the club secretary's daughter. Word had spread of the fantastic German goalkeeper, though much of the interest was curiosity initially, with the war still fresh in everyone's minds.

With Frank Swift now retired, the Blues moved quickly to sign Trautmann after a trial though some City fans were at first resentful of the German's presence in the team, especially as he was the replacement for the revered Swift.

However, he soon won over the doubters, and they were quick to recognise him as a man with the heart of a lion. Incredibly, while helping City to a 1956 FA Cup final victory over Birmingham, he dived bravely at a Birmingham striker's legs and hurt himself badly.

He had, in fact, broken his neck, yet he continued playing, despite the obvious agony from the injury. Doctors later told him that he was within an inch of death, yet he still climbed the steps to collect his winner's medal despite the dangerous discomfort. Such heroism will never be forgotten and some years later at his testimonial, a huge crowd believed to be around 60,000 pans, turned up to pay their respects. A true Manchester City legend.

TREBLE

A club of the stature of Manchester City have enjoyed many great seasons but none so far can compare with 2022-23. Winning the Champions League for the first time, Europe's top tournament completed a treble that included the FA Cup and a third successive Premier League title. These were incredible times for those who have long sung 'Blue Moon'.

Playing in their second Champions League final in three seasons City claimed the trophy for the first time. A stunning 68th-minute goal from man of the match Rodri secured victory against Internazionale of Milan before a crowd of 71,412 at the Atatürk Stadium in Istanbul. City had produced the football of the Gods in the semi-final against Real Madrid. Having drawn the first leg 1-1 in Spain two goals from Bernardo Silva added to by Manuel Akanji and Julian Alvarez provided a fabulous 4-0 second leg win that many a good judge thought was one of the best team performances ever seen by any club!

Bayern Munich had been beaten 4-1 on aggregate in the quarter-final with RB Leipzig beaten 8-1 on aggregate in the round of 16 when Erling Haaland scored five in a 7-0 second leg victory. Earlier City had breezed through the group stage leaving Borussia Dortmund, Sevilla and Copenhagen in their wake. In the FA Cup City did not even concede a goal until a very harsh penalty was awarded against them for handball in the final.

Nonetheless City inflicted a 2-1 defeat on Manchester United with two strikes from Ilkay Gündogan, the first of which after just 13 seconds was the quickest ever in a Wembley final. Seventeen goals had been scored without reply along the road to Wembley.

One of the teams knocked out of the FA Cup were Arsenal. Arteta's Gunners were the surprise package of the Premier League, keeping City off top spot for most of the season until the closing stages when the sheer consistency and relentlessness of Guardiola's team wore them down with a 3-1 win in London and 4-1 home win in April in the head to heads making it crystal clear who the best team in the Premier League were.

77	MINUTES PER PREMIER LEAGUE GOAL FOR ERLING HAALAND - THE BEST IN PREMIER LEAGUE HISTORY.
72%	WIN PERCENTAGE 44 WINS FROM 61 GAMES.
63.6%	AVERAGE POSSESSION PER MATCH
35,142	PASSES IN 61 GAMES
2.5	GOALS PER GAME WITH 151 IN ALL COMPETITIONS
28	ASSISTS IN ALL GAMES BY KEVIN DE BRUYNE
27	CLEAN SHEETS

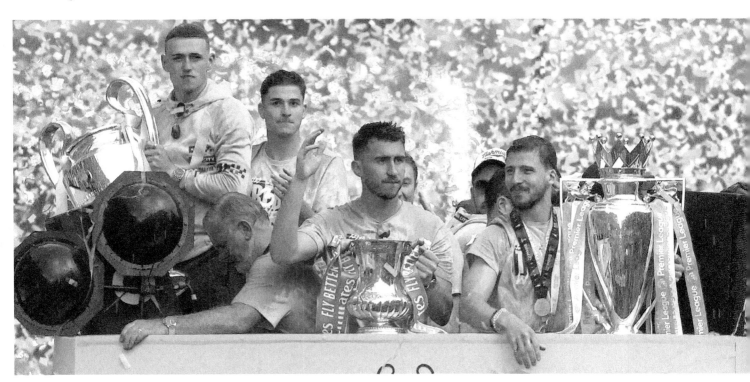

THE VICTORY PARADE THROUGH MANCHESTER, JUNE 2023

TUEART

Signed by City boss Ron Saunders in March 1974, Dennis Tueart became the club's record signing when he arrived from Sunderland for £275,000. The fiery winger soon settled into the side and it wasn't long before he became a big crowd favourite, with his aggressive, never-say-die attitude complementing his dazzling skills and an eye for a spectacular goal.

If he was popular going into the 1976 League Cup final against Newcastle, he came out of it all but immortal after his spectacular overhead kick won the game 2-1. A penalty expert and scorer of several hat-tricks - three in one season - Tueart was a particular favourite among the club's younger fans. Never one to allow the grass to grow under his feet, he left for New York Cosmos in 1978 and again

became a hero to the vast crowds that crammed into the Meadowlands Stadium, in the Big Apple. A Tueart goal would be welcomed by the electronic board message of 'Sweet Feet' or 'Do It, Tueart!'.

Playing alongside some of the world's best players and living a life of luxury, complete with Cadillac, Tueart enjoyed almost two years in the USA before he rejoined City for £150,000 and came back to his adopted home of Manchester for good. Over the next three seasons, he scored 22 goals in 66 starts, this despite a serious Achilles injury. He left the Blues in 1983 as part of a wage-trimming exercise, bound for Stoke, as the club faced up to life in the second division. He returned to the club for a third time in 1997 as a City director and was on the board until 2007.

UEFA CUP

Now the Europa League, City's first foray in the UEFA Cup, formerly known as the Fairs Cup, was in 1972-73 when they took on Spaniards Valencia at Maine Road. The game ended 2-2 with goals from Ian Mellor and Rodney March. The second leg ended the Blues' interest in the tournament with a 2-1 defeat and it wasn't until four years later, in 1966-67, that the Blues again bowed out in the first round, this time to the all-conquering Italian side Juventus.

A solitary goal, courtesy of a Brian Kidd header, was never going to be enough against a superbly organised side and there were no surprises when the Blues lost 2-0 in Turin to crash out of the competition. At least City could console themselves with the fact that Juventus went on to win the trophy. The first round curse continued the following year when Polish side Widzew Lodz held City 2-2 in the first leg and 0-0 in the second, ousting City on the away goals rule.

By far the most enjoyable UEFA Cup campaign came during season 1978-79 when City saw off Dutch side FC Twente and then confidently dispatched Belgian side Standard Liege to set up a tantalising clash with AC Milan. The Blues sensationally went 2-0 ahead through Paul

Power and Brian Kidd. Milan fought back for a 2-2 draw but the result was heralded as one of the best in Europe by an English side and, inspired for the return game, City won 3-0. German outfit Borussia Monchengladbach were next up in the quarter final but after they earned a 1-1 draw at Maine Road, the tie seemed all but over and so it proved as the Germans won the second leg 3-1 and just as Juventus had done before, City's victors would go on to win the UEFA Cup.

In 2003 the Blues qualified for the UEFA Cup via the Fair Play League. EB/Streymur, FC Midtjylland and AC Omonia were beaten as the group stage was reached. City then topped the group which included Paris St Germain after which FC Copenhagen and Aalborg were defeated before City bit off more than they could chew when faced with Hamburg in the quarter-final.

With the competition renamed the UEFA Europa League City took part in 2010-11 in a campaign remembered for City fans adopting 'The Poznan' after meeting Lech Poznan but interest in the competition ended after losing to Dynamo Kiev in the last 16. In recent years City have been European regulars but in the modern era it has been the Champions League that has occupied City and become the Holy Grail.

EMMANUEL ADEBAYOR SCORES FOR CITY IN THE UEFA EUROPA LEAGUE GROUP STAGE MATCH AT LECH POZNAN, NOVEMBER 2010

VARADI

Imre Varadi became a Manchester City cult hero during his two-year stay with the club. He made his debut in a 2-1 defeat at Chelsea, scoring City's only goal and immediately showed the predatory skills the Blues had been lacking. With youth team product Paul Moulden partnering Varadi, the pair inspired a four-match unbeaten run for the Blues albeit City couldn't avoid the inevitable relegation back to Division Two.

With a return of nine goals from a dozen starts, Varadi started the 1987-88 campaign as first choice striker on merit and by this time was proving a huge hit on the terraces. Some say the chanting of his name led to the inflatable banana appearing at Maine Road for one home game and thus followed a chant of 'Imre Banana'! Typically, the mercurial Varadi was sidelined for the 10-1 mauling of Huddersfield Town and found it difficult to break back into the side thereafter. When he did it took him three months to score again and in 1989 he returned to one of his former clubs, Sheffield Wednesday.

W WALKER

One of the fastest full-backs in Europe, Kyle Walker was City's third signing of summer 2017, arriving on a five-year deal from Tottenham Hotspur. Taking the number two shirt, the England international made the right-back slot his own and won six trophies in his first two seasons.

Since his arrival at City, Walker has been a near constant presence. He made his 100th City appearance in the 2019 FA Cup final, reaching the milestone in less than two years. An impressive debut campaign saw him win his first senior honours, the Carabao Cup and Premier League, and he went one better in 2019, adding the Community Shield and FA Cup to his medal collection.

With 42 appearances in 2019-20, Walker again showed consistency, athleticism and remained a vital cog in City's attacking defender ethos. He was at his very best in 2020-21 and made 42 appearances and, like John Stones, won his England place back in the process. A supreme athlete and competitor, a series of injuries restricted him to just 31 starts in 2021-22, though he more than made an impact throughout another title-winning campaign.

Walker's impact early in the 2022-23 season was interrupted by a groin injury. However, after a period of recovery, he was named in the England squad for the 2022 World Cup finals. He went on to make three starting appearances at the Qatar showpiece, helping England reach the quarter-finals before being edged out by France.

Walker was a powerful force at right-back in the latter months of the 2022-23 campaign, helping City secure their third consecutive Premier League title. He also provided experience in City's backline who secured the Double following their 2-1 win over Manchester United in the FA Cup final. He was dismayed at being dropped for the Champions League final against Inter but came on as a second-half substitute as City won 1-0 to win the Champions League and complete the dream of winning the Treble.

WATSON

When you hear people at matches say 'they don't make them like that anymore ', chances are they are thinking of footballers such as Dave Watson.
A mountain of a centre-back, Watson was signed from Sunderland in 1975 where he had earned the unusual distinction of being a full England international without ever playing in the top division.

The towering defender took no time to settle at Maine Road where he formed a tremendous partnership with skipper Mike Doyle, particularly during the 1976-77 season, which saw City come within a point of winning the First Division title. Watson was 28-years-old when he signed and, fortunately for City, the following four seasons would prove to be arguable the best of his career.

Commanding in the air and crunching in the tackle, Watson presented a formidable challenge for any forwards in England and would win a further 30 England caps while at Maine Road before being eventually sold to German club Werder Bremen during Malcolm Allison's second spell at City. In 2020 it was announced that Dave was suffering from dementia.

WEAVER

Nicky Weaver wrote his name into the history books of Manchester City with his meteoric rise that took him to the verge of full England honours during his first few years at the club. Weaver played a vital role in City's successive promotions to the Premier League and became a household name as he saved a penalty that won the 1999 Play-Off final against Gillingham.

His celebratory run saw him skirt the challenges of several teammates before being felled unceremoniously by Andy Morrison. A regular in the England Under-21 team, Weaver was at his best as the Blues raced to promotion from Division One in 1999-2000 but his form dipped the following campaign and he was forced to share first team duties with Carlo Nash. Weaver then suffered a succession of career-threatening knee injuries that saw him miss the best part of three years before revolutionary transplant surgery in America saw him come back in 2005-06 and enjoy a successful loan spell at Sheffield Wednesday. His dramatic turnaround in fortunes came full circle when he seemed to have established himself as first choice keeper again during the 2006-07 season, with his form as good at any time during his career. His popularity never wavered during his ten years with the Blues but the signing of Andreas Isaksson, plus the emergence of Joe Hart and Kasper Schmeichel meant his chances were limited and Weaver finally quite City for Charlton Athletic in the summer of 2007. He went on to join, Dundee United, Burnley and Aberdeen as well as making a return to his home town team Sheffield Wednesday.

A JUBILANT NICKY WEAVER AT THE END OF THE DIVISION 2 PLAY-OFF FINAL PENALTY SHOOT-OUT VICTORY OVER GILLINGHAM, MAY 1999

WOMEN

Manchester City Ladies were formed in 1988, winning their first match against Oldham Athletic on the artificial surface then used at the Latics Boundary Park. With Colin Hendry appointed President in 1990 City were one of the first clubs to officially affiliate with their women's side.

City progressed in the women's game but it was the creation of the FA Women's Super League in 2010 that gave the Ladies game a massive lift to the point now where it is a major sport. On 23 January 2014 the club was renamed Manchester City Women's Football Club.

This was commemorated by the club's first major trophy later that year as they won the FA WSL Cup final beating Arsenal 1-0 in the final at Wycombe's Adams Park with a goal from Isobel Christiansen. Having won the FA Women's Super League in 2016, the Women's FA Cup followed in 2017, 2019 and 2020 with the final being reached again in 2022.

W

WOOSNAM

There have been few sporting all-rounders produced in Britain that could match the man they called 'Gentleman' Max Woosnam. He joined City from the famous amateur side Corinthians in November 1919, and this was his first professional club. A Cambridge Blue at golf, tennis and football, he also won a Wimbledon doubles title and an Olympic gold medal for tennis.

Popular, and the perfect gentleman, hence the nickname, he even on occasion carried a handkerchief around the pitch to befit his image. Born in Liverpool, the handsome, strapping defender immediately gave City's backline a classy look and he never gave less than 100 per cent - the drive that had made him such a winner in so many different disciplines. Well groomed, immaculately dressed and respected by all, Woosnam was a huge success with the City fans and went on to captain both City and England.

He was also a pioneer of amateurs being allowed to play with professionals, increasing his popularity even more within the game, especially when he took a stand against the Amateur Football Association over the matter. He broke his leg on a fence that surrounded Hyde Road in 1922 and in October 1925 he left for Northwich Victoria, having made a lasting impression on the Blues.

X-TRA TIME

Extra time has been both kind and cruel to City over the years. One of the first memorable instances was when the Blues locked horns with Portuguese side Academica Coimbra in the quarter-final of the European Cup Winners' Cup. With no goal scored in either leg, extra time was almost up at Maine Road when Tony Towers struck with just seconds remaining to send City through to the semi-finals.

The 1981 FA Cup final went into extra time too, but despite the Blues having the better chances, the score remained 1-1 and went to a replay (the first at Wembley) which Tottenham Hotspur won with a memorable solo goal from Ricky Villa.

City's dramatic, comeback in the 1999 Play-Off final against Gillingham ensured an extra half-hour of play, often forgotten amid all the chaos, but it passed without either side really threatening and the Blues instead triumphed on penalties. It was a similar tale in the 2016 League Cup final as Liverpool were beaten on penalties.

YOUNG

Gifted, elegant and a wonderful footballer are descriptions attributed to Neil Young during a glorious career with Manchester City. Young played a number of key roles in the City forward line before Joe Mercer gave him the No 10 shirt for keeps and then contentedly sat back as the Manchester-born striker began to fulfil his considerable potential.

Young, better known to the City fans as 'Nellie' possessed a lethal yet cultured left foot and was a key member of the City side that swept all in its path in the late Sixties and early Seventies. In fact, it could be argued that Young had a more substantial role than anyone else during that era, having scored crucial goals at times when important matches were finely balanced.

He was also top scorer when the Blues last lifted the Division One championship trophy with 19 and bagged a couple in the final and deciding game at Newcastle United. It was Young's left-foot cracker that won the 1969 FA Cup final against Leicester City and he was, without doubt, a major influence in City's European Cup Winners' Cup triumph a year later after scoring and then winning a penalty in the 2-1 win over Gornik Zabrze.

Young was mystifying overlooked at international level but his place with the heroes of yesteryear is guaranteed among all Blues followers, many of whom still refer to him in revered tones. Young signed for Preston in January 1972 for £48,000 after 13 years at Maine Road and, sadly, passed away in February 2011 aged 66.

ZABALETA

Pablo Zabaleta played 333 games for City between 2008-09 and 2016-17, 287 of those appearances being starts. As well as a Community Shield game in 2012 Pablo played in four cup finals, being on the winners' side against Stoke in the FA Cup in 2011, and Sunderland and Liverpool in the 2014 and 2016 League Cup finals but being a runner-up against Wigan Athletic in the 2013 FA Cup.

Zabaleta was a model of consistency over his nine seasons. Four times he played in over 40 games in a season with every other campaign bar 2015-16, when he played 22 times, seeing him top 30 appearances.

Capped 58 times by Argentina for whom he played at the 2014 FIFA World Cup Pablo was also a gold medallist at the 2008 Olympics where he played all six games. He had commenced his senior career in his home country with San Lorenzo where he played in midfield rather than in the right back berth he made his own in Manchester. After eight goals in 79 games he moved to Spain with Espanyol in 2005 after captaining Argentina to the 2005 FIFA Under 20 World Cup.

More silverware came Zabaleta's way in his first season in Spain as Espanyol defeated Real Zaragoza in the final of the Copa del Rey while the following season he appeared in the final of the UEFA Cup against Sevilla who took the trophy on penalties. After three seasons in which he scored three times in 102 games City came calling with an offer the player preferred to a counter-offer from Juventus. Zabaleta came to the club the day before the Abu Dhabi United Group led by Sheikh Mansour bought the club. Z might close the alphabet but Zabaleta arrived at the beginning of a new story.

Printed in Great Britain
by Amazon

37798225R00073